ANTHROPOLOGICAL PAPERS

MUSEUM OF ANTHROPOLOGY, UNIVERSITY OF MICHIGAN

NO. 39

RULES OF DESCENT
Studies in the Sociology of Parentage

BY

GUY E. SWANSON

ANN ARBOR

THE UNIVERSITY OF MICHIGAN, 1969

PREFACE

THIS study is one of several. In each of them I explore a particular feature of social structure, and of a cultural system, each feature being chosen because it has special importance for relating the personalities of individuals to the total societies in which they live. We know a great deal about kinship, and about societies, families, and personality. We need to bring all of this knowledge into an increasingly unified framework of explanation. That framework is my long-term objective.

One could, for my purpose, work from individuals out toward the society or from the society back toward individuals. One could do both. Here I work from society toward individuals.

Most of what I say in these pages concerns societies and their systems of kinship. I hope later to present some evidence that bears on implications of this study for our understanding of families and of personalities.

I am grateful to my colleague Horace M. Miner for his generous encouragement, advice, and criticism during the development of this study, to David F. Aberle and Leon H. Mayhew for trenchant reviews of an earlier draft of this report, and to two agencies of The University of Michigan that freed my time for research and that provided research assistance: The Center for Research on Social Organization (a facility of the Department of Sociology) and The Mental Health Research Institute.

CONTENTS

Rules of Descent	1
A Larger Significance of Rules of Descent	5
A Classification of Regimes	12
Descent and Regime	30
Patriliny and Pastoralism	32
Bilaterality	36
Descent in Literate Societies	53
Discussion	74

Appendices

I.	Coding Procedures	85
II.	Ethnographic Bibliography and Summaries	102

Literature Cited	137

RULES OF DESCENT

A rule of descent affiliates an individual at birth with a particular group of relatives with whom he is especially intimate and from whom he can expect certain kinds of services that he cannot demand of non-relatives, or even of other kinsmen.

Descent . . . merely refers to a cultural rule which affiliates an individual with a particular selected group of kinsmen for certain social purposes such as mutual assistance or the regulation of marriage (Murdock, 1949, 15-16).

Like other social norms, the rules governing descent are jural in character: they concern rights and obligations: for example, the right or obligation to help or receive help, to inherit, to exchange gifts, to visit, to celebrate, to name, to have a name, to consider marriage or copulation with certain persons (but not with others), to share a residence and social intimacy, or to exercise authority or to accept it.[1]

Rules of descent are jural principles for assigning individuals to units of kinship that are wider than the nuclear family and whose members are related by consanguineal ties: ties of blood or of common ancestry. These units of kinship may take form as decision-making groups or as unorganized aggregates of people. The members of any unit may live near one another or be dispersed. The unit itself may be structured as a clan, moiety, phratry, kindred, lineage, gens, extended family, or whatever. Its structure may embody some combination of these forms. In almost every society, membership in one or more of these units is an ascribed right and an ascribed obligation for every individual, and in every society, membership entails further rights and obligations. There are, however, wide variations among societies in the character, scope, and importance of these consanguineal arrangements.

Each member of a consanguineal system is affiliated with it through his parents and in no other way: affiliated, that is, through parentage — through his being the child of particular parents, through his parents being the children of particular parents, and so on. Through these bonds, a system of descent provides a continuous framework linking the positions that people hold within a particular nuclear family — and in a particular generation — to the positions they hold in a wider net of kinship.

---

[1] The first extended systematization of rules of descent as jural relations appears in Radcliffe-Brown, 1935. This treatment has subsequently been elaborated by several writers, among them: Fortes, 1953; J.C. Mitchell *in* Southall, ed., 1961; Murdock, 1949:14-16; Sahlins, 1965.

The meaning here of parentage — hence of descent — is social and not biological (Rivers, 1924:86).

An earlier generation of anthropologists completely misunderstood rules of descent, assuming that they meant a recognition of certain genealogical ties to the exclusion of others, e.g., that a matrilineal people is either ignorant of, or chooses to ignore, the biological relationship of a child to its father. Science owes a debt to Rivers for pointing out that descent refers only to social allocation and has fundamentally nothing to do with genealogical relationships or the recognition thereof. It is now known that the Hopi and most other societies with matrilineal descent do not deny or ignore the relationship of a child to its father and his patrilineal kinsmen. ... A number of Australian tribes ... follow patrilineal descent while specifically denying the existence of any biological ties between father and child. In Africa and elsewhere, moreover, it is common for the illegitimate children of a married woman by another man to be unquestioningly affiliated by patrilineal descent with her husband, their "sociological father" (Murdock, 1949:15).

Parentage thus involves the social assignment of some persons as "children" to others as "parents." Rules of descent specify the parent through whom an individual is affiliated with a consanguineal unit: a patrilineal rule specifying affiliation only through the individual's father and through his father's male ancestors, a matrilineal rule specifying affiliation only through his mother and through his mother's female ancestors, a bilateral rule specifying affiliation equally through both of his parents and through their ancestors of both sexes.[2]

It is only rarely that one finds a system of kinship of which all major components can be described under the identical principle that governs descent (Murdock, 1949:258):

... i.e., one in which marriage, family organization, kin groups, exogamy, kinship terminology, and rules of residence, inheritance, and descent have all been brought into complete consistency with one another ...

Murdock reports, for example, that bilateral descent among primitives is most likely to be associated with a patrilineal rule of inheritance and with a matrilocal, avunculocal, patrilocal, or matri-patrilocal rule of residence. He discovered that almost 40 per cent of societies having neolocal or bilocal rules of residence have matrilineal or patrilineal rules of descent, and that a similar percentage of societies having a primarily patrilocal rule of residence lack patrilineal descent. Approximately 30 per cent of societies governing residence by a matrilocal or avunculocal principle employ bilaterality to order relations of parentage (Murdock, 1949:38, 59).[3] Such evidence indicates that form of descent can be empir-

---

[2] A few societies have duo-lineal descent, both matrilineal and patrilineal principals being in force. On the social reasons for children having both a mother and a father see Parsons, *in* Parsons and Bales, eds., 1955 *b*.

[3] But the degree of independence between aspects of kinship has more recently been reduced by more refined classifications. See: *Ethnology*, 6 (April, 1967). Contrary to some theorists, the establishment of family units on a consanguine basis does not almost inevitably lead to an emphasis on unilinear descent. On conditions governing the rise and structure of bilateral or unilinear kin groups, consult: Befu, 1963; Befu and Plotnicov, 1962; Davenport, 1959; Dole, *in* Dole and Carneiro, eds., 1960; Fortes, 1953; Freeman, 1961; Fried, 1957; Ikawa, 1964; Leach, 1962; J.C. Mitchell, 1961; William Mitchell, 1965; Murdock, 1949: 56-64, 1960, 1964; Romney and D'Andrade, 1964; Sahlins, 1961; Sheffler, 1963; Titiev, 1956, 1957.

ically, and not merely analytically, independent of the formative principles that describe other components of a society's system of kinship.

There can also be substantial independence between principle and practice. Sahlins reports that a primitive society's rule of descent may be disregarded in that society except on the rare occasion when it serves as a formal criterion for settling some dispute (Sahlins, 1965). There is further, and recent, evidence that the strength of familial ties of middle class youth in England, in French Canada, and in the United States, especially the strength of familial ties of daughters, is greater to the mother and her kin than to the paternal line, this despite the fact that descent in all three societies seems firmly bilateral.[4]

Such observations suggest that a rule of descent is not directly rooted in the practices of individual families, however prevalent those practices may be. It may instead be grounded in the society at large. This is Sahlins' conclusion.[5] It is shared by Schneider and Homans:

... The kinship system occupies a unique place in any culture, since it is almost always the context within which most socialization takes place. If the dominant values of a culture are to be transmitted and if the culture is to continue beyond the lifespan of any individual, then new recruits to the society must be taught that culture. The dominant values of the total culture must find expression in the kinship system, and they must be so expressed that they can be conveyed to children ... The first social system in which an individual acts is the reduced system of kinship. If he learns the lessons of kinship, he can go on. Kinship must therefore teach him more than the limited scope of pure kinship; *it must teach him the fundamentals of his whole culture.*

... The kinship system as a whole is ... a socialization device, a "child-training practice," if you will, which looms considerably larger than any given child-training practice like weaning or toilet training or aggression control. ... Where it may be difficult to place an exact socialization value on weaning as such, it is much less difficult to discover the socialization values of a whole kinship system.

... the American kinship system embodies in clear and communicable form the essence of the dominant values of the whole culture even while it manages to discharge those functions universal to kinship systems ... (Schneider and Homans, 1955: 1208).[6]

---

[4]Among the more important works are these: Cumming and Schneider, 1961; Firth, 1961; Garigue, 1956; Hagstrom and Hadden, 1965; Lancaster, 1961; Lewis, 1963; Robbins and Tomanec, 1962; Schneider and Homans, 1955; Sweetser, 1963. For a somewhat different perspective, see: Farber, 1964: Chapter 6; and *in* Farber ed., 1966.

[5]Sahlins, 1965. He speaks of principles of descent as a species of political ideology developed by societies.

[6]Schneider and Homans are among the many writers who believe that, in the most advanced societies, the gradual removal from kinship systems of primary responsibility for many other functions (e.g., economic production, religious celebrations, the diagnosis and cure of disease, education for a specific occupation, corporate control of property that is economically or ritually significant) has revealed that socialization and the sharing among kinsmen of intimacy and good will are essential functions of kinship. For related discussions, see: Adams, *in* Dole and Carneiro, eds. 1960; Axelrod, 1956; Brown, 1952; Burgess and Locke, 1950: Chapter I; Farber, 1964: Chapters 1, 4, and 7; Fortes, 1953; Lancaster, 1961; Litwak, 1960a,b; Ogburn, 1929; Parsons, 1943; Parsons, *in* Parsons and Bales eds., 1955a; Rossi, 1965.

What "dominant values" are "embodied" in rules of descent? We can guess but we cannot know. The fact that these rules are present in all societies prevents our testing hypotheses that depend upon their being present in some and absent in others. But we can hope to answer related questions that bear closely upon the first: What values are embodied in matriliny? In patriliny? In bilaterality? (These three varieties of descent are by far the most common and will be the ones of concern here.)

In a previous study I suggested an interpretation of descent by means of which one might answer these questions, and I there examined data to check its adequacy for interpreting matriliny and patriliny. (Swanson, *in* Reiss, 1968). In the pages that follow I apply this same interpretation to bilaterality, sketching only such parts of my earlier work as seem necessary to extend it.

A LARGER SIGNIFICANCE OF RULES OF DESCENT

We know that rules of descent refer to rights and duties derived from parentage and that these rules have their origin outside given families. My proposal is this: Rules of descent express the characteristic form that is taken by processes through which a society fits men to participate in its organization and through which it maintains their fitness for participation across the whole span of their lives. These processes usually take the form of socialization or of social control or of some combination of these two.

I mean by socialization the training of people to participate in their society with increasing skill and commitment. (An assumption underlying socialization is this: it is both necessary and possible that people lacking them be trained in certain skills and be encouraged to adopt certain commitments.) I mean by social control any influence exerted by a society on socialized persons to employ the skills they have learned and to support the commitments they have accepted, this despite their personal tendencies not to do so. (Social control rests on the assumption that compliance with social demands can be obtained, but not a whole-hearted acceptance of those demands.) I see these two processes as inhering in all social organizations, either the one or the other predominating in some organizations; both having a relatively equal status in other organizations. Matriliny, I propose, symbolizes the predominance of socialization in the relations of a society to its members; patriliny the predominance of social control; bilaterality an integration of socialization and social control such that it preserves each while uniting them.

In my earlier research I elaborated on these two processes and connected them with matriliny and patriliny in the following way:

> Systematic study has shown that women are everywhere the chief socializers of the young. This does not mean that men fail to love children and to share in their training. It means that, in all societies, women, most obviously mothers, sisters, grandmothers, and aunts, are held especially responsible for the early care and training of children. They also have special responsibility for reintegrating dissident members of the family, for making them wholly at one with their kin. These seem to me the tasks of socialization.
>
> The special tasks of adult males are what Bales has called the work of "task leadership." A part of that work is the relating of the family, or of other groups, to the environment from which they must obtain their resources. A second part of task leadership is legitimated by the first. It consists of the exercise of necessary discipline over members of the group encouraging, altering, directing, cajoling, coercing. That discipline cannot be exercised as socialization. The group must be coordinated and effective despite deviant desires among members. Socialization may be employed over the long run and may serve to decrease the

amount of discipline required, but, in the short run, the discipline exercised has primarily the character of social control.

... Matrilineal rules of descent arise in societies in which the social system relates to individuals through socialization, the rule symbolizing the system as socializer. Patrilineal rules of descent arise in societies in which the social system relates to individuals through social control, the rule symbolizing the system as an exerciser of social control.

Accordingly, I concur with Schneider and Homans in seeing a society's system of kinship, including its rule of descent, as "a child-training practice" but as designed for all of a society's members — adults equally with youngsters (because both are a society's "children") — and thus as teaching them "more than the limited scope of pure kinship."

What is the "society" that socializes or controls? I mean by a society that organization through which a population makes ultimate and legitimate decisions.[7] The decisions are ultimate in the sense that decisions by no wider sovereignty — no wider political order — can legitimately modify or legitimately condition those decisions. This identifies as the boundaries of a society the province of a population's social machinery for administering a "rule of law." In a system like that indigenous to the Navaho, it identifies each village as a society because, despite great cultural similarities among Navaho villages, there existed within each but not among them a customary or institutionalized apparatus for formulating and implementing legitimate decisions. My definition associates the boundaries of Nuer society with the vague, fluctuating, but customary lines of affiliation by which small segments of a population — ordered in this case by kinship and residence — may form associations for mutual aid in war or another emergency, these lines of of affiliation constituting normatively recognized dependencies of varying strength if not quite constituting normatively sanctioned bonds of obligation. This conception of a society identifies the limits of a modern national polity or of a unified primitive state with the legitimate scope of its central government and with the many political processes through which that government is sustained and its decisions implemented. To summarize, I think of the society in a population as identical with the normative and organizational system through which that population is enabled to take action, however minimal. I take as the most representative expression of that society whatever norms and organizations explicitly serve a people as their widest legitimate polity.

It is not uncommon for a society to have a somewhat different organization in time of war or other major crisis. In the United States, for example, the powers of the President increase and some civil rights are curbed. For purposes of analysis, I shall consider as a society's polity the system used in times of peace.

When I think of a society socializing its members, or exercising social controls over them, I have in mind relations between this political system and the adults

[7]Discussed in Swanson, 1960:42-44.

who are members of the society. (I am not here concerned with the socialization or social control of children by adults.) I propose that systems of descent symbolize the socialization or social control of a society's members — adults and children — by that society. I further propose that the relative weight that a society gives to socialization or to social control depends upon the possibility and necessity of socialization.

As I have defined it, socialization is possible to the extent that people can progressively be shaped to fulfill their part in their society's undertakings: trained in the relevant skills and persuaded to adopt and fulfill the relevant commitments. Socialization is impeded, and social control made likely, to the extent that people can rightfully pursue special interests that compete or conflict with the interests of their society — with the "common" interest.

It is true that all men have special interests and serve them, but it is also true that, in some societies, the political system legitimates this pursuit of special interests whereas, in other societies, only the common interest may rightfully be advanced. Special interests are legitimately pursued to the extent that people are authorized to participate in their society's political system as members or agents of somewhat autonomous groups within the society. When this is the case, I anticipate a stress on social control. In some societies, however, political participation is rightfully undertaken only in one's status as a subject or agent of the society as a whole. In those societies, I expect a stress on socialization. To illustrate the difference I turn to examples from Europe in the sixteenth century:

> In the sixteenth century, Venice was an independent city-state and the supreme authority in Venice was its Great Council. This council had to approve all important policies of government. It served as the highest legislature and highest court. It also served as the highest executive, selecting all important officers of the state, requiring that they be responsible to it, defining, on occasion, the policies which those officers might pursue, and allowing most important officials to hold office for very short and non-renewable terms — terms of from two to twelve months. The point significant for us is that all males who were full citizens of Venice were members of the Great Council. I think this point important because it indicates that participation in the operation of the Venetian (political) . . . system was open to men in their capacity as members of the society at large and not because of any traits thought peculiarly theirs as individuals or as representatives of particular groups in the . . . (population).
>
> Consider, for contrast, another city-state of the same period, the Swiss canton of Zurich. In Zurich, the supreme authority was again a council, its powers closely resembling those of the Great Council in Venice. Its membership, however, consisted of representatives elected by the several mercantile and artisan guilds into which the whole population of male citizens was divided. Under this system, a role in the central operation of the . . . (political) system was open to men only in their capacity as representatives of organized groups, those groups not being themselves agents of the system but, rather, . . . (autonomous organizations in the population).
>
> Consider now the relevance of socialization and social control for these contrasts between Venice and Zurich. In Venice, men participated in government on the grounds of what they had in common with all other members of the . . . (society) and it was exactly

the purposes they had in common that had given rise to the . . . (society) itself. Moreover, in Venice, certain formal controls were applied to insure that persons in responsible positions would not use those positions for personal rather than common advantage. Among those controls were short non-renewable terms of office and the responsibility of the officials to the Council. It is perfectly true that in Venice, as everywhere else, each member of the . . . (political system) had some interests and purposes peculiarly his. In this sense there were special or selfish interests rather than common interests. But, in Venice, the institutional structure provided no legitimate place for the exercise of those special interests in determining who would govern or in what cause government would be conducted. The Venetian . . . (political) system was, in this sense, insulated from the effects of special interests. Moreover, in their operation of the . . . (political) system, participants were defined by this system as essentially sympathetic to it. They had much to learn about its needs. They would need to be trained and corrected. They must come to discriminate with increasing precision between the system's requirements and their own. But, given their basic commitment, their continued life within the system and their service both to it and from it would produce steady improvement in these matters. This steady improvement, I suggest, is appropriately considered a process of socialization.

In Zurich, matters were different. Men participated in government to support the common undertakings on which all depended, but they participated only if they also served and supported special interests . . . – the guilds – making certain that the . . . (political) system served those special interests as well as the common interest. . . . men related legitimately to the . . . (political) system in a manner which indicated that their special interests were not foregone in pursuing the common undertakings. Indeed this structure recognized that those special interests were organized, perpetuated, and fueled by groups . . . having a considerable autonomy. I suggest that processes then emerged which may appropriately be considered processes of social control. Participants in operating the . . . (political) system might, in its name, coerce and encourage and implore and seduce one another's support for the system and, because the system was important to all, they often were successful. On the other hand, they had always to reckon with the presence in their fellows of persistent, ineradicable special interests and with the likelihood that such interests would conflict with those of the common enterprise. The most that could be achieved would be an ever-strengthened accommodation between the two concerns founded on an increase in the individual's commitment to the importance for him of the common interest and his determination and skill in helping to control such of his own desires as conflicted with the common interest. (Swanson, *in* Reiss, 1968:105-107)

In these examples, we have societies in which ultimate authority resides in the whole citizenry. In many societies, however, an individual – for example, a chief or king – or a small, self-perpetuating group – perhaps a council or oligarchy – performs the ultimate executive, judicial, and, sometimes, legislative functions. I call such an individual or group a governor. A governor's powers will almost always be justified as being exercised in the common interest. Societies having a governor are found to differ in the extent to which members or representatives of somewhat autonomous groups in the population may rightfully share in the exercise of the governor's powers or in the implementation of the governor's programs. To the extent that a governor rightfully monopolizes governmental functions, the polity provides for the pursuit only of common interests, and, I anticipate, the society will stress socialization. The greater the degree to which persons who serve special interests may rightfully share in the governor's exercise of his powers, the greater, I anticipate, will be the society's stress on social control.

To summarize: In earlier research on descent, I proposed that social control, hence patriliny, will characterize a society's influence over its members to the extent that those members are able institutionally to participate in its political system — in its ultimate, decision-making processes — as agents of special interests and that socialization, hence matriliny, will characterize a society's influence over its members when they can rightfully participate in its political system only as agents of the common interest. (I intended these generalizations about descent to apply only to the simpler societies. I discuss more complex societies later in this report when I apply the foregoing theory to societies having a bilateral rule of descent. The city-states of Venice and Zurich are among those societies.)

In introducing the ideas of socialization and social control, I said that the relative weight given to one process or the other depends upon the possibility and necessity of socialization. To this point I have discussed differences among societies with regard to the possibility of socializing their members. What of cases in which socialization is unnecessary or, at least, is less necessary?

There are societies — those that I describe more fully below, employing the label "unitary centralism" — in which most of the members are subordinated not only under a governor but under two or more layers of officials whom he appoints. These members have a legitimate political role only as the hands and feet of a governing apparatus — what I later call a "technical" role. There consequently is little concern over the spontaneity and wholeheartedness of their service but only with their performance of that service. In this kind of society, socialization is not as necessary as it would be were it required that people be personally committed and involved. I therefore expect a stress on social control in unitary centralist societies.

base in such ultimate factors of sovereignty as membership—this is the Hegelian element. In either distinguishing from bureaucracy in that it operates with a specific constitutionally decreed ultimate element, are performative. It differs from bureaucracy in the exercise of a constituting order, and in particular, as of representative of, special subjects to the process, but in particular, as representative and reflectionism. The Venetian organ — rhetoric reflectionism only. It in neither distinguishing from bureaucracy in that it does —

As this point, and before we pass on to Cell D (centralism), we can note descriptive: "But of of this subordinate cluster, Nothing in these first three types of relate performance for cases of dissent. Nothing in these first three types of where seen to make centralization necessary. But in case of these, it would be effects on centralism. Both planetary and heteronomy are political systems wide the right of contestants and firmly to pursue their special interests. Centralization is a product system that provides no formal place for such ind-lay, it disavows value laws, except the simple implicit, performance and uniformity and a performance more of dissent, commission as mandatory rule. The relevance of dissent to centralism varies because, as we shall find, there are several, impressively different, types of centralism.

The fourth cell, Cell D, is labeled "centralism." This is to represent the extreme in some fashion of an individual or small group — a Caesaric extending the executive and perhaps the judicial and legislative functions of government. Thus exercise of authority is legitimate when conducted on behalf of the social system. Thus these functions of government are summarily defined as enclaved only for the common good or in the common interest. They are specifically not performed or conducted for other interests, for special interests, investigating and effectuating in the special service of interests in the domestic or a centralist regime is a differentiated part of the policy which consequently are performing of ultimate factors. The position of interests re-

A CLASSIFICATION OF REGIMES

I have been illustrating political conditions that might be related to socialization or social control and thence to rules of descent. Illustrations are not enough. We need for our purpose a typology of political systems — of regimes — designed systematically to identify those polities in which the pursuit of special interests is legitimized, and those in which it is not. Figures 1, 2, and 3 serve these purposes. Figure 1 provides a general paradigm. Figure 2 employs that paradigm to generate a classification of regimes. Figure 3 expands the classification of Figure 2.

Figure 1 refers to social relations within any social organization, a society being one possible example.[8]

	Association	Social System
Elements	A	C
Parts	B	D

Figure 1. Relations among participants in an organization.

Let us assume that, unless otherwise coerced, participants stay in any organization for the sake of things they get from doing so. No assumption about social relations seems safer than this, that men form organizations and preserve them for the benefits those organizations provide their participants. On this assumption, organizations are associations among their participants. This is the notion coded in the first column of Figure 1.

But there is a second, equally safe, assumption: Although men may undertake among themselves a series of exchanges and joint efforts, they quickly discover that these are possible only if special attention is given to the maintenance of their relations to one another: to the solution of problems of coordination and control; to the devising of standards by which decisions can be made, disputes resolved, and plans implemented. Men come, in short, to be

---

[8] For a definition of an organization and for a discussion of the paradigm that follows, consult my paper (Swanson, 1968). Discussions by others of some ingredients relevant for this paradigm include: Parsons, Bales, and Shils, 1953: 66-67 and Chapter 5; Parsons and Smelser, 1956: 36.

not only the founders and users of an organization but its supporters and agents as well. As supporters and agents they must act on behalf of the organization's needs if it is to persist and prevail, that persistence and success being a condition for the fulfillment of their own desires. To the extent that participants in an organization so identify whatever is required for the maintenance and promotion of their organization, and to the extent that they act on behalf of their organization, we speak of their being not merely persons in association but members of a social system. The second column of Figure 1 codes this development.

It seems obvious that most, perhaps all, organizations are at once associations and social systems, that their participants are simultaneously users and agents of an organization, and that this inherently dual status of participants often places them in a quandary: their personal desires are likely on many occasions to conflict with the needs of their organization and, in any case, the pursuit either of their personal interests, or of the "common interest" of the social system, is necessarily undertaken at some cost to the other. Because each participant is both a user of his organization and an agent acting on its behalf, these intra-organizational conflicts are, for him, intra-psychic conflicts. Socialization and social control represent two methods by which an organization can influence the outcome. Before elaborating that point, we should consider other ideas relevant to it, these being contained in the rows of Figure 1.

Depending upon the source of the facilities they employ, participants in an organization have status as elements in the organization or status as its parts. "Facilities," Parsons (1951:72) reminds us:

> ... are possessions in a special mode of significance to action; they are positions devoted to the "production" of further "utilities." that is, destined to be used as means to some future goal rather than as objects of immediate gratification. Regulation of rights to facilities or access to them, and of the possibilities of the acquisition of these rights through exchange is therefore another of the fundamental functional problem foci ...

Participants in an organization are elements in it to the extent that they possess, apart from this particular organization, properties relevant for interaction in it — for example, their personal characteristics, their roles in other social groups, their material possessions, their control over space. Thus workers in a factory are elements in that organization with respect to age, native energy, intelligence, political views, and the like: all of these being characteristics they would possess were they not employed by this particular organization. Participants in an organization are also and simultaneously parts of that organization, this to the extent that they have properties that are theirs only as participants in this particular organization. A workman's seniority is such a property, it being typically dependent upon his length of service with a particular employer. More generally, what, in the narrow sense of the word, are called a man's "roles" are his properties as a part of some organization.

To summarize: The whole of Figure 1 represents any organization. The columns identify the principal ends that may be served as determined by the inherent duality of a social organization as an association and as a social system. The rows identify the means to which participants in an organization have access because they are (a) inherently within the organization (parts) yet (b) do not cease being the actors who existed prior to the organization and who have a continuing status independent of that organization and outside it (elements). The four cells in Figure 1 give us relations that men in an organization may have to one another, these relations varying according to the ends participants serve and the means participants dispose.

I have said that every organization is at once an association and a social system and that participants in it are at once elements and parts. In every organization, all of these features are to some extent legitimated. We have seen, however, that the objectives sought through an association will sometimes be incompatible with those sought through a social system. In every organization, one set of objectives — or the other — comes normatively to have precedence if the two sets are in conflict. Organizations differ in which set has precedence.

Likewise, in every organization, there is some normative definition of the extent to which people are allowed, or required, to participate as elements or as parts. (From the participants' point of view there are advantages and disadvantages either way. If he is an element, a person is encouraged to make available facilities that he independently commands. Possession of such facilities gives him the advantage of a greater freedom of action. But participation as an element entails a disadvantage: it requires that a participant put some of his own resources at the disposal of the organization, thereby making them unavailable to him for other purposes. Participation as a part entails the opposite set of attractions and disadvantages.) Organizations differ in treating participants primarily as elements or as parts.

Figure 2 is based upon Figure 1 but no longer refers to a single organization. Instead it contains a classification of organizations in which they are arranged according to the precedence they give to the pursuit of their participants' interests as members of an association or as members of a social system and according to their definition of participants primarily as elements or as parts. Organizations are thus classified according to their basic political arrangements: their regimes.

Cell A is now labeled "heterarchy." In heterarchy, an organization consists — for the making of ultimate, legitimate decisions — of two or more separate but formally equal participants, the participants or their representatives coming together for discussion and decision. Their objective is the satisfaction of their respective special interests, perhaps of a common interest as well. To that end they employ facilities they would possess even were they not members of this organization. The Winnebago Indians afford an example. Among these people, ultimate, legitimate decisions were made at the level of the tribe. The heads of the constituent clans met together and, as a council, made tribal policies. (There was a tribal chief, but he had little official power.) Each clan was a separate organization having its own traditions and its own apparatus for managing its internal affairs and supporting tribal activities from its own resources. These clans were elements because each had resources under its independent control and each needed some of the resources from the others as facilities for the conduct of their common enterprises. A second example of heterarchy, already given, is that of the regime in medieval Zurich. In Zurich, the guilds had the status of elements.

	Association	Social System
Elements	A Heterarchy	C Commensalism
Parts	B Heteronomy	D Centralism

Figure 2. Types of polity.

Cell B is now labeled "heteronomy." The Nuer and many other stateless or segmentary peoples have this type of regime. So also do those peoples among whom observers report no form of government to exist and no means for making binding decisions or for enforcing decisions. In these latter societies individuals do come to work together but only on the basis of their consent as individuals. It is common that observers describe these peoples as highly individualistic, perhaps irascibly so. Two features of these societies are of special importance. In each there is a "rule of law" in the sense that many norms exist which govern peoples' rights and obligations once their interaction begins. In each there is lacking a continuing organizational apparatus for making decisions or a political apparatus having a specified membership. There exists, instead, the appreciation by participants that they are more closely linked by kinship or territorial proximity to some of their fellows than to others. When in need of collaborators, they call first upon these "neighbors" for help. There may be no normative rule specifying that such requests should be honored. There are, however, strong pressures upon "neighbors" to assist if they are later to mobilize assistance for themselves; and there are, once assistance is contemplated, norms governing the establishment and operation of these ad hoc relationships.

It is correct to associate with Cell B certain properties of a market situation after the manner conventional in economic analyses. Participants are assumed to be seeking their own goals. They find, however, that others do likewise and that there emerges a pattern of dependencies among all participants which gives to each the properties of his position in the pattern itself. As is well known, the status and properties of an economic "dominant" are of this sort, those properties not being characteristics of the person involved, but becoming his by virtue of his position in the market situation. They are his because he is a part of that situation. The position in these simple polities of being a closer "neighbor" of some participants than of others is of the same sort.

The term "commensalism" in Cell C refers to regimes in which all adults or "free men" — that is all adults with full civil rights (or some representative subset of these adults, perhaps all adult males or all males over 30 years of age) — possess, when meeting as an assembly-of-the-whole, ultimate authority for making decisions. A commensal polity differs from heterarchy in that men participate in making ultimate decisions in their capacity as members-at-large of the society, not as participants in, or as representatives of, special subgroups in the population. It differs from heteronomy in the existence of a continuing organization with a specified membership through which ultimate decisions are legitimately made. It is further distinguished from heteronomy in that at least some such decisions are binding and enforceable. The Venetian regime — already described — had all of these characteristics.

At this point, and before going on to Cell D (centralism), we can note certain implications for rules of descent. Nothing in these first three types of regime seems to make socialization unnecessary, but, in two of them, it would be difficult or impossible. Both heterarchy and heteronomy are political systems built upon the right of individuals and groups to pursue their special interests. Commensalism is a political system that provides no formal place for such activity. I therefore expect that, among the simpler societies, heteronomy and heterarchy will be associated with a patrilineal rule of descent, commensalism with a matrilineal rule. The relation of descent to centralism varies because, as we shall find, there are several, importantly different, types of centralism.

The fourth cell, Cell D, is labeled "centralism." This is to represent the existence in some polities of an individual or small group — a governor — exercising the executive and perhaps the judicial and legislative functions of government. This exercise of authority is legitimate when conducted on behalf of the social system. Thus these functions of government are commonly defined as conducted only for the common good or in the common interest. They are specifically not legitimate if conducted for other interests, for special interests. The governor in a centralist regime is a differentiated part of the polity having prerogatives and obligations originating in the special service it renders in the making and implementing of ultimate decisions. The position of governor is, thus, a special role or part designed to serve the requirements of operating a social system.

Level of Decision	Means	Ends	
		Association	Social System
Policy	Elements	Balanced	
	Parts	Balanced	
Managerial	Elements		Limited centralism
	Parts		Feudalism
Technical	Elements		Simple centralism
	Parts		Unitary centralism

Figure 3. Types of Centralism.

Figure 3 is an expansion of centralism. It is based upon the fact that the governors of some centralist regimes share their powers with certain persons, or with subgroups, these having independent rights in formulating the regime's decisions or in formulating the procedures by which those decisions are implemented. For example, a tribal chief may serve as a governor but may have to share his authority in decision-making with a council consisting of hereditary or elected representatives of the regions into which the tribal territory is divided. Perhaps the concurrence of these representatives is required before certain of the chief's decisions can take effect, or perhaps the representatives choose the officers who implement the chief's decisions. Figure 3 classifies centralist regimes according to the level of decision-making, if any, at which some members of the polity have such an independent share in the governor's powers. The more significant their share, the greater is the opportunity for them to shape the regime's policies to serve interests peculiar to themselves or the subgroups they represent.

A governor's powers may be shared at the level of central policy making or at some lower level of administration. As we know from the discussion of Figure 2, participants in heterarchic or heteronomous regimes operate at the highest levels of those polities, pursuing there — and by right — both their own special interests and the common interest. Participants in commensal regimes also operate at the highest levels of policy making, but have a legitimate place in that process only as agents who serve the common whole — the common interest. In Figure

3, policy-making is distinguished from other levels of administration in centralist regimes.[9]

"Policy" refers to the highest level of authority and decision. In centralist regimes, the governor is located at that level as are any other persons, hereditary or elected officers of state, who have in their own right some share in the highest powers. The "technical" level in Figure 3 refers to subordinate levels of government to which policies are applied. "Managerial" refers to a level of government that links to the highest center of policy formulation, levels that are lower still. The managers may be directly incorporated into the central state apparatus as line officials of a central bureaucracy or they may be the line officials at the head of the major territorial divisions of the state. In the simpler centralist societies there is little or no development of a managerial level. Perhaps, for example, a chief deals directly with all village heads, villages being the only units subordinate to him. In that circumstance, management occurs, but it must be performed by the chief and by the heads of villages with the result that the three levels – policy, managerial, and technical – are not sharply separated from one another in the structure of the polity. Indeed, it becomes apparent that policy and technical functions are distinguished in a polity to the extent that management – the activity which separates policy-making from technical activities – is itself distinguished from both.

I begin with the regime at the bottom of Figure 3. A unitary centralist regime is one in which the governor alone may legitimately formulate the central executive and administrative policies and implement them. For example, the governor may on its own authority appoint major administrative and judicial officers, raise armies and militia and direct their use, decide upon the proper expenditure of taxes and aids, establish and operate a system of courts, and direct foreign affairs. In a unitary centralist regime there is a clear distinction between managerial and technical functions, this being embodied in the existence, in the "line"

---

[9] These levels are adapted from Talcott Parsons' discussion in Parsons, (in Parsons, ed., 1960). Every social organization relates instrumentally to an environment. That environment consists of "materials" – that is of resources and of conditions for obtaining them. In any organization, however simple, there are technical activities, these having to do with the obtaining of resources and with so processing them that they can be utilized by the organization and its participants. Similarly, there are managerial activities, that is, activities which allocate, coordinate, control, and support technical activities. Finally there are policy-making activities. These consist of efforts to determine what technical activities should be performed, to allocate resources among them, to determine the distribution of the processed materials they produce, and to evaluate the relative support deserved by various kinds of technical activities at a given period of time.

Although all organizations contain all of these activities, in only some organizations are some or all of them separately organized. The usual discussions of an organization's "evolution" picture differentiations of that sort. An inspection of the code employed in this study reveals that I employed such differentiations in a more refined manner than is indicated in Table 3. The additional refinements were included to make easier the tasks of coding even though many of the refinements were not immediately germane to the theory being tested. I especially depended upon the following discussions for those refinements: Southall, 1953: 241-263; Apter, 1955:86-99, Apter, in Hoselitz and Moore, eds., 1963; Swanson, 1967; Fortes and Evans-Pritchard, eds., 1940:1-23; Eisenstadt, 1959; Sahlins, 1963. The single most important reference was Hinsley, 1966.

organization of the state, of at least two hierarchically ordered operating levels that direct the administrative and/or judicial activities at lower levels. Officers of at least two such managerial levels are designated by the governor. This, as we shall find, was the pattern in classical China and in many of the native kingdoms of East Africa, that in Ganda providing a well known instance (Murdock, 1957). The entry in Figure 3 should be read as follows: In unitary centralist regimes, men other than the governor participate legitimately in the formulation and implementation of a society's policies only in a technical capacity or as managers appointed by the governor.

Immediately above in Figure 3 is a regime called simple centralism. In this kind of regime, as in unitary centralism, only the governor or its agents may legitimately operate at the policy or managerial levels. But here the managerial level is not well developed in the structure of the state: there is only one level of management appointed by the governor or he himself performs most managerial functions. As a consequence there is a less sharp distinction between technical and managerial functions, the persons or groups that perform technical functions having also to undertake managerial activities. This usually means that, relative to those in unitary centralist states, the technical levels of a simple centralist government have a greater discretion about how they conduct their work and a wider sphere of competence over which to operate. The result is that they have more the status of elements: they have greater independence of the governor and he has to take more account than would the governor of a unitary centralist polity of the preferences of his subordinates at the technical level.

In a feudal regime, the next in ascending order in Figure 3, there exist both technical and policy-making bodies. Between is a managerial stratum. This stratum has independent control over levels below it, and that control may take many forms. With reference to the superordinate policy level, however, feudal authorities are the lowest level of government. This curious situation is readily illustrated in the classic feudal systems in medieval Europe. In those systems, a king or other supreme lord had in principle, often in practice, exclusive authority over the central executive and judicial operations of the state. His vassals were pledged to obey his lawful orders, obtaining in return his protection, the order he enforced in the kingdom, and, perhaps, some claims to economic assistance. It is true that a supreme lord gained legitimate sway over subordinates only with their consent and upon his agreement to afford them stated services, but they became his vassals only with his agreement and they were then bound to serve as his agents in implementing his lawful orders. Thus, with reference to the overarching polity of the state, these vassals constituted the lowest political unit. The vassals themselves might, and often did, have vassals and other dependents, although these were not the vassals or dependents of the supreme lord. Thus the vassals of a supreme lord were his subordinates and agents and were, simultaneously, independent lords over their own subordinates. They therefore are coded as operating at a managerial level of government but, with reference to the central state, as having status only as its parts.

In limited centralism (see Figure 3) there is again a managerial stratum. Its position differs from feudal vassalage in two respects: (1) All free men in the society are equally subordinates of the governor. (2) The governor's agents, like the local authorities in simple centralism, must enforce central policies but, being constituted by some process independent of the governor, they have powers the governor does not fully control. This is the situation when, for example, regions or provinces or clans provide an intermediate level of administration and when their governments, although obliged to accept and implement policies determined at a higher level, consist of hereditary officials or of persons selected by locally-controlled procedures. To implement its policies in such situations, a governor must temper those policies to what it knows to be the likely disposition of its managers to implement directives from above.

In Figure 4 are summarized patterns of answers to three questions by means of which one can distinguish among unitary centralism, simple centralism, limited centralism, and feudalism. As the figure indicates, there are two distinct patterns that lead one to judge that a society is unitary centralist. (The appropriate sub-pattern of unitary centralism is designated for societies coded later in this report.)

There are, finally, in Figure 3, regimes I have called balanced. In these, some individuals or groups in the society have significant autonomous powers and normatively, and as a consequence of their powers, have a share in the governor's central operation of the government. Thus in some societies the governor must make its policies with the consent of hereditary heads of clans or of regions, or with the consent of representatives chosen by such persons. When the councillors are elected representatives, they often are responsible to their constituents as well as to the governor. As Figure 3 indicates, involvement by such autonomous authorities at the level of policy-making introduces, at that level, authorities who have independent powers in the society's association. Those authorities may act as members of that association and not merely as participants in the society's social system. (There are perhaps different varieties of balanced regime depending on whether their autonomous units are elements or parts, but I have not found occasion to employ such refinements in my work and do not indicate them in Figure 3.)

How, in the simpler societies, are the various types of centralism related to rules of descent? A governor's powers are always legitimated as being exercised in the common interest. We have seen, however, that centralist regimes differ in the extent of those powers and in the degree to which they must be shared with autonomous persons and groups. Special interests have, by normative provision, a large share in the powers of the governor of a balanced regime. There-

A.	Characteristics		No	Yes
	1. Does the governor designate the persons who, at two or more operating levels in the polity (e.g., central bureaucracy, regions, provinces, villages), direct administrative and/or judicial activities at lower levels?		0	1
	2. Is there some operating level of administration and/or justice intermediate between the lowest level and the highest over which persons or groups have rights and powers independent of the governor's?		0	1
	3. Do the governor's rights and powers extend in some or all important matters of administration and/or justice to all free men? (In some societies "all free men" will mean families, villages, or other groups, they, and not separate individuals, having political rights.)		0	1

B.	Patterns		Characteristics		
			1	2	3
	1. Unitary centralism	a.	1	1	1
		b.	1	0	1
	2. Simple centralism		0	0	1
	3. Feudalism		0	1	0
	4. Limited centralism		0	1	1

C. A note on other patterns: We do not find under B (above) three of the eight patterns of characteristics that might be generated from combinations of three dichotomous characteristics taken three at a time. A positive answer to question A 1. (above) is always accompanied by a positive answer to question A 3. A negative answer to A 3. would confuse unitary centralism with feudalism were the pattern 1-1-0 and would involve a contradiction were the pattern 1-0-0 (a governor appointing two or more levels of supervisory officials who serve as the exclusive line-organization of the state yet who have no power over the people who must ultimately implement the state's policies). The pattern 0-0-0 would present the contradiction of there being a full-fledged governor who had no means of exercising his authority.

Figure 4. Characteristics that distinguish four types of centralism.

fore, I anticipate that such a regime will be associated with a patrilineal rule of descent. In simple centralism, the governor alone may legitimately formulate executive and administrative policies and initiate their implementation. On my assumptions, simple centralism should therefore be associated with matriliny. Does this mean that unitary centralism should likewise be associated with matriliny? I think not. I think that matriliny symbolizes a relationship of socialization between a society and its members. I think that socialization is possible under both simple centralism and unitary centralism, but that it is unnecessary under unitary centralism.

Socialization, I have said, requires that people be progressively shaped to undertake their society's tasks: that they come to acquire and to exercise the necessary skills and commitments. Socialization is possible under simple centralism. Why is it also necessary? After all, people who legitimately have a political role only at the technical level of government are defined as those to whom policies are applied. Unlike policy-making or management, the technical level does not entail the making or modification of policy. This is true by definition. But, under simple centralism, there is an additional and critical fact: although having only a technical role in their regime, people are conceived as elements. This means that they must use facilities they independently control — for example, their skills and commitments — as the means for carrying out the policies that they are obliged to implement. People in that circumstance must be reinforced in their commitment to do what is expected — they must come to serve spontaneously and wholeheartedly — and must be trained and retrained in the coordination of their own efforts with those of others. Such reinforcement and training — both directed toward the service of the common interest — is a process of socialization.

By contrast, under unitary centralism, people placed at the technical level are conceived to have a legitimate political role only as parts. This means that they not only serve the common interest — and it alone — but that they have no independent control over the means by which that service is executed. As I noted earlier, the spontaneity and wholeheartedness of their service is therefore of no concern. They are conceived solely as objects to which policies are applied. (And perhaps in unitary centralist regimes it is this transformation of people into objects that explains why a casually brutal discipline is so common in the dealings of their elites with subordinates.) In these circumstances, socialization is unnecessary. To underscore the point: As conceived under unitary centralism, people have no legitimate political role that would suggest that they could be anything but wholehearted in their service. Socialization being unnecessary, I would then expect social control to be emphasized.

Feudalism and limited centralism are "between" simple and unitary centralism on the one hand and balanced regimes on the other. In each of these two cases, there exist important kinds of managerial autonomy that are associated with local interests and restricted to local affairs. In my first research on descent, I was not certain which pattern of parentage should be associated with feudalism and limited centralism, and I was able to avoid the problem because no society in my samples appeared to have such a regime. The problem later became critical when I was planning the study of bilaterality that is described farther on in this report. I shall leave for consideration at that point any further discussion of the relationship between rules of descent and feudalism and limited centralism. I turn now to methods and results of the earlier studies that served as preparation for my work on bilaterality.

DESCENT AND REGIME

My first research on descent involved only matrilineal and patrilineal societies. I had then in hand a classification of regimes on the order of that in Figures 2 and 3 and reasoned approximately as follows:

1. Rules of descent institutionally express the style of parentage predominating in relations between a society and its members, those relations being at least in part embodied in a society's regime. Matriliny expresses socialization as a style of parentage; patriliny expresses social control.

2. Parentage will take the form of socialization unless a society's members can, of right, participate in its regime in the service of special interests. If they can legitimately participate in the service of special interests, parentage will take the form of social control.

3. Members of societies having commensal or centralist regimes are empowered legitimately to participate in those regimes only as members and agents of their society. Therefore parentage in those societies will take the form of socialization and the rule of descent will be matrilineal. (In this first study I had not come to distinguish unitary centralism from simple centralism or either of these from feudalism. "Centralism" here means all of these.)

4. Members of societies having heteronomous, heterarchic, and balanced regimes (and, to a lesser extent, members of societies having limited centralist regimes) are empowered legitimately to participate in those regimes in the service of special interests. Therefore parentage in those societies will take the form of social control and the rule of descent will be patrilineal.

To evaluate this reasoning, I drew a sample of 40 primitive societies from Murdock's World Ethnographic Sample — 20 matrilineal societies and 20 patrilineal societies, these being chosen at random within the constraints that they be matched so far as possible for culture area and for their chief means of obtaining sustenance. (Given this rule for obtaining matching pairs of matrilineal and patrilineal societies, one has to take one's cases from four world regions: Africa, the Pacific islands, North America, and South America. The means of sustenance will be what Aberle calls dominant horticulture or "other horticulture": these societies lack the plough and they depend upon the cultivation of crops but not upon the rearing of large animals as a major source of subsistence.) The codes for culture area, means of subsistence, and rule of descent were taken from Murdock. (1957:664-87). I read the ethnographic reports and coded the regimes. Assistants who knew nothing of the problem under study employed the same code in reading reports for 24 societies in the sample.[10] Their coding

---

[10] I received skilled help in various phases of this work from Wendy Hartley, Carla Shagass, Barbara Milsten, Patricia Marcoux, and Billie Lawson.

of regimes agrees with mine in 83 per cent of the cases. I present my original coding in Table 1a and my assistants' in Table 1b. It is evident that there is a very strong relationship of the kind expected between descent and regime. It is also evident that this result is produced primarily by societies coded as commensal, centralist, and heterarchic or heteronomous, there being at most, one limited centralist regime and only three balanced regimes.

Table 1a
REGIMES AND LINEALITY

Rule of Descent	Type of Regime				
	Commensal	Centralist	Limited Centralist	Balanced	Heterarchic or Heteronomous
Matrilineal	7	12	0	0	1
Patrilineal	0	3	0	3	14

Table 1b
REGIMES AND LINEALITY

Rule of Descent	Type of Regime				
	Commensal	Centralist	Limited Centralist	Balanced	Heterarchic or Heteronomous
Matrilineal	5	6	1	0	0
Patrilineal	1	1	0	3	7

This result was encouraging and sufficed for the purposes with which I began. I knew, however, that this classification of regimes was inadequate for explaining the existence of a patrilineal rule of descent in some societies that fell outside the constraints employed in drawing this first sample, and I had yet to determine what code might be adequate for explaining the further variance that bilateral rules of descent would introduce.

PATRILINY AND PASTORALISM

It is well established that almost all societies depending heavily or primarily for sustenance upon the raising of large animals have a patrilineal rule of descent[11]. Such societies were excluded from my first sample. What are their regimes? By the time I addressed this question, my classification of regimes included all those in Figures 2 and 3. My theory had also been expanded, now including the further ideas about patriliny and regimes that appear below. Among those ideas was the judgment that one must distinguish unitary centralism from simple centralism, the first being associated with a patrilineal rule of descent, the second with matriliny.

I knew, from general reading, that two patrilineal societies were clearly "centralist": Ganda and classical China. A comparison of their political structure with that of societies I had found to be matrilineal and centralist led to a new distinction: Ganda and classical China had what I subsequently termed "unitary centralism." (I found by reanalyzing the data in Table 1 that the centralist matrilinies had simple centralism.)

I have suggested one reason for a relation between unitary centralism and patriliny: the reason being that, under unitary centralism, socialization is unnecessary. There may be another. I derive it from a consequence of unitary centralism: the development within it of a new, institutionalized basis of deviance from central control.

Perhaps the point about unitary centralism important for patriliny is this: control of technical operations by policy-making authorities occurs through the development of a subservient but differentiated managerial level. To the extent that technical operations are seen to be different from policy-making, they — and the managerial activities above them — come to have a kind of independence from policy-making and policy-makers, the technical and managerial authorities necessarily defining and employing certain standards required by their special tasks. Those standards will complement the instructions given by policy-makers but will frequently limit policies or conflict with them. (Nothing is more familiar in the historical evolution of bureaucratic organizations.) By this reasoning, the extension of centralist control generates exactly that which it was designed to overcome: institutionalized special interests. Under unitary centralism these special interests arise as specific procedures for serving the

---

[11] For reviews of the literature and original findings, consult: Aberle, (in Schneider and Gough, 1962); Hobhouse, Wheeler, and Ginsberg, 1915; Murdock, 1937; D'Andrade, (in Maccoby, ed., 1966).

common interest, but they may come in time to promote only one part of that interest, and hence they become competitive with each other and with the whole of the common interest.

Of the two arguments just given, one, both, or neither may be correct. In any case, I decided to distinguish between simple and unitary centralism and to see whether this distinction would help to explain the presence of patriliny in pastoral societies.

The sample drawn for this purpose consists of 15 of the societies that are coded in the World Ethnographic Sample as depending upon the rearing of large animals for their dominant or co-dominant means of obtaining sustenance. I purposely included the two pastoral peoples — the Tuareg and Ngoni — shown in the Sample as non-patrilineal. The remaining 13 societies were chosen to maximize the diversity of the cultural areas that were represented. A coder unacquainted with my interest in rules of descent read the ethnographic reports on all 15 societies and coded their regimes. Her code agrees with mine in all but one instance. (I coded the Kalmuk regime as heteronomous.) Table 2 contains her coding of these societies. (Appendix II contains a summary of relevant ethnographic data for coding each society.)

Table 2
DESCENT AND REGIME IN PASTORAL SOCIETIES

Regime	Rule of Descent		
	Matrilineal	Bilateral	Patrilineal
Heteronomous* or Heterarchic			Buduma* Dinka* Fulani* Kazak Lugbara* Nuer*
Commensal			Lapps
Balanced			Bedouin (Rwala) Hottentot Swazi
Limited Centralist or Feudal	Tuareg (Ahaggar)	Ngoni (Mpezeni)	Kalmuk (Baga Dorbed)
Simple Centralist			
Unitary Centralist			Nyoro[b] Zulu[a]

Note: a, b are subtypes of unitary centralism coded in Figure 4. See Ethnographic Summaries Appendix II, p. 79 ff.

As the theory forecasts, the regimes of patrilineal pastoral societies tend to be heteronomous, heterarchic, balanced, or unitary centralist. Eleven of the thirteen cases fit this expectation. The one matrilineal society among these pastoralists, the Tuareg, has a limited centralist regime as does the single bilateral society, the Ngoni.

BILATERALITY

If the interpretation given for matriliny and patriliny is correct, can the same line of reasoning be extended to predict the occurrence of bilaterality? It seems on the surface that a bilateral rule of descent represents some combination of matriliny and patriliny. Perhaps it represents some combination of the principles of socialization and social control. But what combination? Murdock (1949: 56) warns:

... bilateral descent ... unlike (double descent) is not a simple combination of patrilineal and matrilineal rules. The distinction becomes clear in examining Ego's relation to his four grandparents. He is aligned in the same kin group as his father's father under patrilineal descent, in the same group as his mother's mother under matrilineal descent, and in different kin groups with each under double descent. In none of these instances, however, does he find himself in the same kin group with either his father's mother or his mother's father. Under bilateral descent, however, he is affiliated equally with all four grandparents, and all four, being secondary relatives of his, will necessarily be members of any consanguineal kin group of bilateral type to which he himself belongs. Bilateral descent, instead of being a combination of patrilineal and matrilineal, reflects a complete absence of any unilinear emphasis.

I proceeded with this warning in mind. I also took advantage of observations gained from previous research and from my reading of reports on a preliminary sample of 15 societies, all of the latter having a bilateral rule of descent and chosen according to the sampling rules employed in obtaining societies for Table 1.

The first point that caught my attention is a matter of common knowledge: with the possible exception of Albania, every contemporary European society has a bilateral rule of descent. (Many of these peoples can trace this rule to Roman times or even earlier[12].)

The second important observation arose in the course of exploratory work: In reading about the bilateral societies in my preliminary sample, I was struck by the fact that the simpler among them, and some of the more complex as well, had a commensal or centralist polity and a communal economy (i.e., an economy in which members of a society have rights to produce from a common store provided through activities of their polity, a store from which they always, or often, get a substantial part of their sustenance). Checking back, I found no case in which a society in my matrilineal-patrilineal sample had a communal economic organization.

---

[12]On the very early history of European kinship, consult: Friedrich, 1966; Goody, 1959.

A third observation also came from this exploratory reading about bilateral societies: among the more complex bilateral societies, some provided clearer instances of limited centralist or feudal regimes than I had found in my sample of matrilineal and patrilineal societies (see Table 1).

I owe a fourth and final observation to my coders who persuaded me to make a distinction among heteronomous societies. Although all heteronomous societies lack the means for making or enforcing binding decisions, the people in some of these societies routinely see a great deal of one another as an assemblage of the whole. This is especially likely in heteronomous societies having small populations, the people living close together and constituting a single community: a small rural neighborhood or a single village or hamlet. All of the people, or at least the adults or the men, spend a lot of time together. They come almost every day to a common meeting place – a plaza, a well, a wharf, a ceremonial lodge. These occasions have some aspects of a town meeting: there is a physical assemblage, not merely an informal network of interpersonal obligations. There may be a collective task involved (e.g., cleaning the plaza, repairing boats) or none at all. Moreover, the people assemble as members of some stable collective organization such as a village or a clan. Members have the right to participate in the assemblage exactly because they are members of the larger whole. No decisions are made or enforced on these occasions, but public affairs are under discussion and there emerges a collective focus of attention and perhaps a collective sentiment concerning them. By this means the commonality of which all are parts is made organizationally salient. I came to think of these societies as having a kind of "commensal" heteronomy and to distinguish them from other heteronomous societies in which these routine collective assemblies do not occur. The latter have an "individuated" heteronomy. This distinction is important because I began to see in my preliminary reading that commensal heteronomy was accompanied by a bilateral rule of descent whereas the heteronomous societies associated with patriliny were usually individuated.

The four observations about bilaterality just reviewed seem to me to have something in common. I will describe it first as found in limited centralism.

Under limited centralism two things are explicitly institutionalized, the form of that institutionalization providing for each a separate and legitimate place yet making the existence of either depend upon the existence of the other. Under limited centralism there is the separate organization for making central policies. Its functionaries have independent resources for the pursuit of their work. The legitimation of their work derives from its serving the society's general interest: from contributing to the society as a social system. But this central organization must implement its policies by employing at the managerial level, and below the governor and his central aides, persons and groups having independently the right so to serve. These latter represent local and special interests even while they implement policies devised to serve the general interest. They act, therefore, both as independent bodies in the society as an association and as agents of the society as a social system. As independent bodies they cannot legitimately define the social system's needs. That is done by the central state organization. But they have of right the power to adapt to their special, local situation policies designed to meet the needs of the society's social system: to adapt these policies to their special interests. It should be stressed that limited centralism does not make separate but equal the social systemic and associational aspects of a society. Rather it structures them as interdependent parts of a single organization: the social systemic aspects comprising the "head" that is helpless without its associational "hands and feet," and the effective pursuit of special interests by local groups being, in turn, impossible without the services of the centrally governing head, the local groups also serving as its agents. In this fashion, I suggest, association and social system, hence social control and socialization, are organized together not as parallel structures but as parts of a single whole.

A limited centralist polity embodies the pattern of relations I take bilaterality to represent. It remains to state more generally the essentials of that pattern and to examine four additional ways in which a society's organization may embody it: in a feudal system, in a differentiated religion, in a communal economy, and in commensal heteronomy.

The essential pattern that bilaterality symbolizes is, I believe, the separate institutionalization of the society's social system and of some requirements of its participants in their capacity as members of its association: some requirements of participants in addition to those they have as agents of the social system itself but requirements which they may legitimately expect to satisfy through participation in the organization that is their society. This institutionalization makes of the society's social system, and of the participants in the association, something other than different and parallel structures: making them rather into complementary, mutually dependent features of a single organization.

In limited centralism, and in certain other societal structures to be described, the subordination of special interests to the common interest is clear. This subordination makes possible some exercise of socialization, special interests having an independent and legitimate status but having to submit to common interests in case of conflict. But this same legitimate independence of special interests means that their submission will not in principle be complete: that social control must also be exercised to coordinate and direct the common effort.

An important facet of these ideas is caught by concepts like *res publica* (the affairs of the people), *jurisdictio* (the rights of private persons to manage their private affairs and to have changes made in their status only with their consent), and commonwealth. Each concept refers to a situation in which the society at large contains an explicit institutional mechanism — a regime or, as we shall see, a differentiated religion — by means of which its citizens can, of right, receive aid in their several individual pursuits (e.g., the pursuit of sustenance, justice, salvation, aid in local affairs). The regime or church is in good part supported because it provides this aid, its legitimation being dependent upon that service. On the other hand, the common interest is also embodied in a continuing institutional structure, and, in cases of conflict, special interests are subordinated to it.

Despite their many differences, a limited centralist and a feudal regime share the broad form of polity I have just described. In a feudal system, an overlord is supreme in command of the executive and of most of the higher judicial functions of the state. He is its "head." But his vassals need not in principle accept his government unless he fulfills his obligations to them: the obligations to provide justice and order, to consult with them before undertaking policies that might commit their resources (e.g., making decisions concerning war and peace), and to protect them from foreign aggression. Similarly, the overlord need not in principle retain a vassal who will not provide the support for the lord's government upon which both have agreed: assistance with the lord's courts, provision of taxes, loans, and aids; provision of military service, and of advice and counsel as requested.

What of the observation that a bilateral rule of descent has been found in almost all European societies (and in those derived from them) at least since the fall of Rome? However one explains this fact, he must recognize that almost all the forms of regime represented in Figures 2 and 3 have appeared since Roman times in one or more of these societies. It cannot be these forms of regime as such that accounts for the pervasiveness of bilaterality. We must look elsewhere for some clues.

When Western scholars contrast their civilization with other high cultures, they usually point to the existence in it of legal and religious institutions independent of the state[13]. Strictly speaking, however, legal institutions gained a certain independence in only a few Western countries and then not until the 17th and 18th centuries. By contrast, the independence of the Christian Church has roots in the thought of Seneca and the Stoics, receiving its explicit, undergirding rationale in the writings of Saints Ambrose, Augustine, and Gregory, and its authoritative formulation in pronouncements by Pope Gelasius I (492-496 A.D.) (Wolin, 1960:124-131; Sabine, 1950: Chapter 10). The position of the Church has in it two features important for our purpose: first, it formally recognizes the legitimate existence of both church and state and, second, it authorizes their organizational separation and collaboration. In what did that separation — that differentiation — consist?

---

[13] For recent surveys of literature on this point, see: Bellah, 1964; Coulborn, 1958; Coulborn et al., 1959; Eisenstadt, 1962; Parsons, 1964; Strayer, 1958.

... Spiritual interests and eternal salvation are in the keeping of the church and form the special province of the teaching conducted by the clergy; temporal or secular interests and the maintenance of peace, order, and justice are in the keeping of civil government ... Between the two orders, that of the clergy and that of the civil officials, a spirit of mutual helpfulness ought to prevail ...

This conception is often spoken of as the doctrine of the two swords, or two authorities ... In doctrinal matters the emperor must subordinate his will to the clergy and must learn rather than presume to teach. It follows that the church, through its own rulers and officials, must have jurisdiction over all ecclesiastics, for obviously in no other way can it be an independent and self-governing institution. (Sabine, 1950:194-95).

To be thus differentiated from one another, two institutions cannot depend solely upon doctrine. Each must have its own guaranteed sources of support. Each must have independent control over the performance of work distinctive to it. A man's position in either must not in principle be the criterion by which he attains a particular position in the other.

These were, in fact, the relations between church and state in Christian societies. The church had lands, tithes, contributions, and endowments independent of the state's sources of support. The church alone determined its basic doctrinal positions and the rituals and practices appropriate for their implementation. The particular position of a man in church or state was not, in principle, the basis for his position in the other: a monarch might be in a state of mortal sin whereas a saint might be without political power; a priest or bishop had, in his sacral capacity, no special role in the conduct of secular government; and a secular overlord had no formal role in determining or correcting the sacral status of a church member or priest. The church operated its own schools, these being almost the only schools then available. Church and state supported and exploited one another, but were nonetheless separated in doctrine and organization.

This development in Christian societies, and in some others, takes us a step beyond the institutional structure of many other highly complex societies. In the more advanced primitive societies, and in non-European societies of very high culture, the state and religion are differentiated from the institutions of kinship and from specialized economic enterprises. In Christian societies, and in a few others, state and church are differentiated from one another.[14]

One further step must be taken to make clear the structural fit between our theory of bilaterality and the existence of a differentiated church. In religions having a differentiated church, Christianity being the prime example, we have

---

[14]In this, Christianity and some other religions differ from any faith, e. g. the religions of classic Greece or Rome, that seeks primarily the welfare of the state or the society as a whole. Later developments of comparable importance in general social evolution include the separation of the legal order from other activities of the state and the separate institutionalization of what medieval writers termed jurisdictio as distinguished from gubernaculum. On this latter point, consult Swanson, 1967: Chapters 2 and 3.

what Bellah terms "historic" religions[15]. In these religions, especially in Christianity, there is conceived to be a gulf between God and his world and, because man's sacral status requires the bridging of this gulf, the effectuation of that bridging — the problem of salvation — becomes a supreme concern. In addition, it is believed in these religions that salvation is something men attain as individuals because it is contingent upon their own individual qualities — perhaps upon the merits of their conduct — and is not, as in other theologies, given to men according to the sacral status of groups to which they belong: families, communities, their society. The church — visible or invisible — is a primary agency in the process of salvation.

I take it to be consistent with the best of our knowledge that the ideas of gods and spirits arise from experiences with the more enduring and often unarticulated traits of societies and of other groups as corporate actors — as social systems.[16] A church embodies those traits in doctrine, organization, and ritual; it systematizes them and rationalizes them. By these means it enables the faithful concretely and coherently to experience the largest realm of meaningful order in which they live and to guide their lives accordingly: to overcome that separation from the divine that is formulated as the problem of salvation.

Whereas a governmental apparatus — a state — deals with the more immediate issues of the polity, serving as its executive machinery, a differentiated church expresses what are thought to be the polity's enduring, meta-constitutional properties. But that church, like that governmental structure, serves and represents the polity and especially the polity as a social system: it serves and represents the common interest, the foundations of societal integration. In its relations with individuals, its function is to relate the enduring common standards and interests and the enduring social order to men's personal needs and to their deviations from the divine will, ameliorating conflicts, facilitating socialization. Because men, while in this world, are considered separated from the divine — as being incapable of full socialization into the divine purpose — the church must also exercise social controls that mobilize men's commitments to the divine order despite their presently insuperable deviations from it. Here again we seem to have the essential pattern I first abstracted from limited centralism and associated with the adoption of a bilateral rule of descent. This time it appears as the institutionalization of the common interest and of the special ego-oriented needs of individuals within an integrated structure and the concomitant institutionalization of procedures by which the society — by means of the church — exercises both socialization and social control.

I propose, next, that the combination of a communal economy and a differentiated political system shares these same abstract characteristics. In this

---

[15] Bellah, 1964:366. See also Parsons, 1966.

[16] For a detailed review of this problem, see Swanson, 1960 and 1967.

instance, the communal economy plays the part served in limited centralism by independent local authorities: it embodies in institutional form personal, hence special, interests of all individual participants in a society. In a communal economy, it is the normal procedure — and not just an emergency arrangement — that every participant in the society has of right a share in the staple foods which that society produces, and there are in force in these economies regularized procedures that embody that right of participants. (There are, for example, norms requiring the immediate sharing of game or the routine setting-aside of some portion of crops for general use.)[17] Although the whole society is strengthened thereby, the immediate needs served are not those of the society itself but of the individuals in its population. They are served by an activity enforced by the society's political processes if not always organized under them.

But a communal economy embodies more. It is an institutional form that makes legitimate not only the demands of individuals upon society but the obligation of those same individuals, as agents of society, to meet their fellows' demands. They must plant and harvest and store and distribute as well as receive and consume. A communal economy thus embodies a society's organization both as a social system and as an association and concomitantly exercises both socialization and social control.

A final embodiment of this pattern is to be found in the form of regime that I have called commensal heteronomy. In this pattern, the special interests of individuals and of families can legitimately be pursued. Indeed, there are no formal collective arrangements for curbing the society's members. There is no apparatus by means of which the members can make collective decisions that are binding. But the people in such a society all live in a single, small community and all, or a large part of them, regularly assemble to talk and socialize. Objectively, these people are heavily dependent upon one another. Objectively, they come to know the common sentiment on most questions and, because it is publicly expressed, people are more likely to judge themselves and one another in terms of that informal collective standard. Thus, under commensal heteronomy, there comes to exist a legitimation of the pursuit of special interests and an expression and legitimation of collective standards, standards that must be taken into account when special interests are being pursued. The special interests and the collective standards are integrated into a single system of personal and collective life, of association and social system.

To summarize, I have proposed that five disparate organizational patterns — limited centralism, feudalism, a differentiated religion, a communal economy,

[17]A communal economy should not be confused with what some economic historians and ethnographers refer to as a "redistributive system". In a redistributive system, all adults in a society are expected to present large gifts to officials of the central government, the officials, in turn, being expected to give public feasts or to make generous presents to the citizens. Under these circumstances, there is a considerable process of indirect exchange of goods, but these goods are given as gifts and what officials give particular citizens is in principle a matter for the officials' discretion, not a matter of the citizens' rights to a particular share in their society's produce.

and commensal heteronomy — have something in common, that common feature being symbolized by a bilateral rule of descent. (Codes that operationalize these ideas and specify them more exactly appear in Appendix I.)

The common feature that I suggest is critical, is the institutionalization, in each of these patterns, of men's rights and obligations as members of their society's association and their rights and obligations as members of its social system. It is probable that still other patterns of social organization also contain this common feature. I have suggested that, in each of the five patterns examined here, these two sets of rights and obligations are both present and integrated. In a communal economy or in commensal heteronomy they may or may not be normatively differentiated. In limited centralism and feudalism, that explicit differentiation has appeared. In religions like Christianity, religious agencies have themselves become normatively differentiated from other institutions and provide within their structures a legitimate place for men's action both as participants in their society's association and as members of its social system. (There must certainly be a connection between evolutionary advance and these societal patterns associated with bilaterality, but an explication of that connection goes beyond the scope of this report and the state of existing knowledge.)

SOME EVIDENCE ON BILATERALITY

These notions about bilaterality were checked against two samples of societies. The first consists of a cross-validation sample of 20 societies all having a bilateral rule of descent and having the characteristics already described for societies in Table 1. The second sample consists of "literate" non-Western societies listed in the World Ethnographic Sample. These two samples are not as large or diverse as one would like, but they provide a considerable range of social complexity and the cases in them come from a wide range of geographic and cultural areas. The first sample has the further merit of being comparable in economic level and geographic-cultural areas to the sample drawn earlier in my study of matriliny-patriliny.

I read and coded the principal ethnographic sources for societies in both of these new samples. Graduate students who did not know the object of my research or the theory employed read the materials for the cross-validation sample. They also read and recoded the ethnographic reports for societies listed in Tables 1b and 2, classifying them according to the more elaborate set of categories employed in studying bilaterality. (None of these readers had been among the original coders for societies in Tables 1b and 2.) Table 4 contains their conclusions. (Their judgments coincide with mine in 70 per cent of the cases: see Table 3 for the details.)

There are 22 bilateral societies in Table 4. One of them, the Ngoni, appeared in Table 2 among the pastoral societies. But one society (the Lapps) that was

TABLE 3
AGREEMENT BETWEEN CODERS

Author's Code	Another Coder's Judgment												
	Heteronomous		Commensal			Heterarchic	Centralist				Uncodeable	N	X
	a	b	c	d	e		f	g	h	i	j			
Heteronomous: a	7	2	...	2	...	...	...	1	...	...	...	...	12	58
: b	...	6	...	...	...	...	...	...	...	...	...	...	6	100
Commensal : c	...	...	7	...	...	...	...	...	...	...	...	1	8	88
: d	...	...	...	6	...	...	...	...	...	...	...	...	6	100
: e	...	...	...	...	1	...	...	...	...	...	...	...	1	100
Heterarchic :	...	...	1	...	...	3	...	...	...	...	...	...	4	75
Centralist : f	...	...	...	...	...	2	4	2	...	...	1	1	8	50
: g	...	...	...	...	...	...	...	2	...	1	...	...	3	66
: h	...	...	...	...	...	...	...	...	2	...	...	...	0	...
: i	...	...	...	...	...	...	...	3	...	4	...	1	10	40
: j	...	...	...	...	...	...	...	...	...	...	2	...	2	100
Uncodeable :	...	8	8	8	1	5	4	6	2	5	3	3	0	...
N	7	8	8	8	1	5	4	6	2	5	3	3	60	...
Y	100	75	88	75	100	60	100	33	0	80	67	0	...	70

Note: *a*-individuated heteronomous; *b*-commensal heteronomous; *c*-commensal; *d*-commensal with communal economy; *e*-commensal with differentiated religion; *f*-balanced; *g*-limited centralist; *h*-feudal; *i*-simple centralist; *j*-unitary centralist; *N*-number of cases; *X*-percentage of author's coding with which another coder agreed; *Y*-percentage of another coder's coding with which author agreed.

TABLE 4
REGIMES AND DESCENT IN SIMPLER SOCIETIES, ECONOMY CONTROLLED

Regime	Pastoral			Horticultural		
	Patrilineal	Matrilineal	Bilateral	Patrilineal	Matrilineal	Bilateral
Individuated heteronomous	Buduma Dinka Lugbara Nuer	...	...	Maricopa Tiv Tucuna	...	...
Commensal heteronomous	Fulani	...	...	Orokaiva	...	Havasupai Iban Lapps Trumai Ulawans Wapishana
Heterarchic	Bedouin (Rwala) Kazak	...	...	Tikopia Winnebago	Pawnee (Skidi)	...
Commensal	...	...	...	Araucanians* Aymara	Apinaye Delaware Navaho New Ireland	Cábaga* Cashinawa* Ifugao* Jivaro* Marquesans* Nicobarese Penobscot* Subanun* Tewa (San Ildefonso) Tupinamba Yaqui (Sonora)†
Balanced	Hottentot Swazi	...	...	Atayal Mende	...	...

BILATERALITY 39

Table 4 (continued)

Regime	Pastoral			Horticultural		
	Patrilineal	Matrilineal	Bilateral	Patrilineal	Matrilineal	Bilateral
Limited centralist	Kalmuk (Baga Dorbed)	Tuareg (Ahaggar)	Ngoni (Mpezeni)	...	Lamba Marshallese	Tonga
Feudal	...	...	...	...	Yao	Taino
Simple centralist	...	...	...	...	Bemba Buka Kongo Zuni	Jukun
Unitary centralist	Nyoro[b] Zulu[a]			Omaha[a]		
Judged uncodeable (inadequate or conflicting evidence)	...	...	...	Fang	Talamanca	Natchez

*Communal economy; †Differentiated religion; a, b- Sub-types of unitary centralism coded in Figure 4. See Ethnographic Summaries Appendix 2, pp. 121 ff.

classified as patrilineal in Table 2 is coded as bilateral in Table 4. What happened was this: After my sample of 20 horticultural, bilateral societies was drawn and my coders had begun to classify the regimes of those societies (and the regimes of societies in Tables 1b and 2 as well), Murdock published (in the journal *Ethnology;* April, 1967) corrections of the code for descent that he had earlier given for certain societies in these samples. I have incorporated his corrections into Table 4, there classifying the Lapps and Jivaro (the latter a society in Table 1b) as bilateral rather than patrilineal, and the Pawnee as matrilineal rather than bilateral.

Of the 22 bilateral societies tabulated in Table 4, seven have a commensal polity and a communal economy, six are commensal heteronomous, one has a feudal regime, two have a limited centralist regime, and one has a differentiated religion. All these findings are consistent with the theoretical expectations as previously sketched. Five societies appear inconsistent with those expectations: three having a commensal regime, one having a balanced regime, and one being uncodeable. None of these five has a communal economy. Appendix II presents a summary of the evidence crucial for coding each of these 22 societies. Table 4 also indicates that coders once again obtained results for patrilineal and matrilineal societies similar to those in Tables 1b and 2. The whole of the results in Table 4 are summarized in Table 5. The relationship between descent and regime shown in that table is strongly in the expected direction ($r = +.86$; $\sigma'_r = .13$).

TABLE 5
REGIMES AND DESCENT IN SIMPLER SOCIETIES

Regime	Patrilineal	Matrilineal	Bilateral	Total
Individuated heteronomous, heterarchic, balanced, unitary centralist	18	1	0	19
Commensal, simple centralist	1	8	4	13
Commensal heteronomous, commensal with communal economy, limited centralist, feudal, differentiated religion.	4	4	17	25
Uncodeable	1	1	1	3
Total	24	14	22	60

DESCENT IN LITERATE SOCIETIES

The societies already considered differ greatly in complexity, ranging from households, tiny villages, and nomadic bands to kingdoms of more than a million people. Table 6 adds another 18 societies to our list. These are all but two of the most advanced non-Western societies in Murdock's Ethnographic Sample — those in which writing was known. (The Aryans and Babylonians were omitted because I could not find adequate information about their political systems.) These societies changed through their long histories and the table indicates the particular historical period for which government and descent are recorded. I retain the periods designated by Murdock. (When Murdock suggested no date at all, I chose at random an historical period for which adequate information on polity and descent was available.) The coding is based on my own reading of relevant sources.

The trend in earlier tables appears once again. One patrilineal society was heterarchic, three were balanced, and six were unitary centralist. One was commensal. Of the societies having a bilateral rule of descent, two had a limited centralist polity, one had a feudal regime, and four had unitary centralism. Among the bilateral societies having unitary centralism, all had either a religion clearly differentiated from the state and from other institutions or had a communal economy. No society that was patrilineal in descent and unitary centralist in polity had a differentiated religion or a communal economy. To summarize, 17 of these 18 societies exhibit the expected relations between descent and other aspects of social organization.

I turn now to a brief description of each society in Table 6, indicating evidence essential for my coding it as I did.

A HETERARCHIC SOCIETY

Just before its conquest by the Spanish, great changes seemed under way in the Aztec state but their outcome is uncertain and we must refer to a period somewhat earlier (the early fifteenth century) to find a more stable, indigenous polity. The principle of Aztec polity was a federation of clans. The tribe consisted of twenty exogamous clans; each clan regulating its own affairs and its leaders representing it on the tribal council for the handling of common problems. The tribal council in turn elected a supreme chief and other officers of

TABLE 6

DESCENT AND REGIME IN NON-"EUROPEAN," LITERATE SOCIETIES

Regime	Rule of Descent	
	Patrilineal	Bilateral
Individuated heteronomous	. . .	. . .
Commensal heteronomous	. . .	. . .
Heterarchic	Aztec (early 15th century)	. . .
Commensal	Athenians (500 B.C.)	. . .
Balanced	Iranians (Sassanid period) Koreans (Yi dynasty) Maya (period of Spanish conquest)	. . .
Limited centralist	. . .	Egyptians (Middle Kingdom) Romans (Principate)
Feudal	. . .	Japanese (Tokugawa period)
Simple centralist	. . .	. . .
Unitary centralist	Chinese (Ming dynasty) *b* Hebrews (Solomon's kingdom) *b* Javanese (1800 A.D.) *b* Sinhalese (Kandyan period) *b* Tibetans (1900-1950 A.D.) *b* Vietnamese (18th century) *b*	Burmese (circa 1800 A.D.) *a†* Cambodians (18th century) *a†* Inca (Imperial period) *b** Thai (18th century) *b†*

a, b - Sub-types of unitary centralism coded in Fig. 4; * - Communal economy;
† - Differentiated religion.

whom it could dispose at any time. The several clan leaders meeting together constituted the governing body of the Aztec state.

There seems no doubt that this democratic polity had begun to change before the Spanish conquest. Supported by a new military elite that was generated through imperial conquests, the tribal leader had become increasingly independent of his council and the Aztec elites had increasingly differentiated themselves from the commoners, obtaining large personal holdings in land and attaining a growing control over public offices and over outward display of prestige as in dress and ornamentation. Nonetheless the Aztec state had not finally crystallized into whatever form it might later have taken and our best estimate of its indigenous structure, even at the time of the conquest, is that of a heterarchic polity.

A COMMENSAL SOCIETY

It is astonishing how much we know about some aspects of Athenian life in 500 B.C. and how little we know with certainty about the government of the state. Athens was by then a city state and the constitutional reforms of Cleisthenes were well established. But there are many gaps in our information about the actual practice of government and administration.

When the people that were later the Athenians first appeared in history, they consisted of four tribes acknowledging a common sacral king. The tribes consisted of phratries and the phratries of gentes and, in each of these units, there were both aristocrats and commoners. In time, pressures from the aristocrats removed the kings from political office, the royal family retaining its hereditary priestly functions but its former role in government being assumed by a noble oligarchy. Access to office and, more generally, participation in government was restricted to persons holding membership in a traditional gens, phratry, and tribe, and being of aristocratic family.

Although the immediate occasion for Solon's reforms is a matter for debate, they were probably inspired by unrest occasioned by these restrictions on participation in government. The major effect of his reforms was to make participation in government dependent upon wealth, not blood. The subsequent reforms of Cleisthenes struck even more directly at the ancient kin groups and their role in politics.

Cleisthenes built his system upon the deme, a traditional territorial unit, rather than upon the gens, a unit of kinship. He divided the Athenian demes into thirty groups of which ten were taken from the city of Athens, ten from inland territories, and ten from coastal territories. Each cluster of ten was called a trittyes. One deme from each trittyes was chosen to make up a new cluster of three demes — the component demes sometimes having contiguous territories and sometimes not — and the cluster comprising a new tribe. There were thus ten new tribes in all. Demes and tribes became units of government incorporated directly into the operations of the Athenian state.

In each deme there was an assembly of all adult male citizens which, by some means, probably election, appointed officers who served for one year. The chief of these officials, the demarchos, had charge of the detailed internal administration of his deme including the maintenance of public order and the carrying out of commands of the Athenian central government. Final powers in all local matters resided in the deme assembly. Membership in a deme was hereditary. As a result of population movements, there might be resident in a deme adult males ineligible to participate in the local assembly but members of another deme's governing citizenry.

Tribes were corporate bodies under a president. All male members were members of the tribal assembly. This assembly passed on decrees which fell within their competence including those concerning the tribal cult. Each tribe supplied one regiment of the Athenian army, members of the tribe serving together under their own officers. The tribal assemblies selected officials, the assemblies retaining full powers of government should they desire to exercise them.

The central Athenian regime had two principal organs: an assembly and a council. Membership in the assembly was open to all adult males born of Athenian parents. The assembly met in Athens several times a year, electing all magistrates, approving taxes, passing legislation, serving as the highest court, receiving ambassadors, deciding upon war and peace, and retaining final control over all other actions of government. As might be expected, attendance was heaviest among citizens living in or near the capital.

But the assembly's powers were not without restriction. It was not to consider any unlawful action, for example an action to abandon the constitutional structure designed by Cleisthenes. Its president (elected for a single sitting of the assembly) was not to permit the consideration of such an action and its secretary was not to enregister such motions. More than this — and although the assembly retained final powers — all actions by the assembly were to be referred to the council for its opinion.

The council consisted of 500 men, 50 being chosen from each of the ten tribes and apportioned among the demes of a tribe according to the relative population of each. Councilmen were selected by drawing lots from among the candidates who presented themselves for office: candidates who met the formal qualifications regarding citizenship in a deme, and who passed an examination of their character by the council in office. (Even after councilmen came to be paid for their service by the state, the wealthier citizens were more likely to attain this post.) A councilman's term of office was one year and he could have no more than two terms.

The council elected its own officers, these being chosen in equal numbers from the several tribes and restricted to terms of one-tenth of the year. Working committees were chosen by a show of hands or by the drawing of lots. Having been thus constituted and organized, the council set to work, meeting frequently and, on most issues, developing recommendations before submitting a topic to the assembly.

No city-state the size of Athens could function without an executive-judicial branch. The council and assembly performed some of these functions but the day-to-day activities were conducted by magistrates. These were chosen by lot from candidates put forward by the demes and tribes. Magistrates served for a year and had to have their powers reinstated by the Athenian assembly on nine occasions during that year.

These many innovations did not include the abolition of the four ancient tribes or of their phratries or gentes. They survived to perform ceremonial and religious functions, and membership in a phratry was still a condition for Athenian citizenship, the current members, as in times past, having to vote their acceptance of new members. It is still unknown how these traditional units were prevented from rejecting persons otherwise qualified to be Athenian citizens. The common scholarly opinion is that their approval must have been reduced to a formality.

Whatever its ambiguities, this Athenian polity is a clear exception to our expectations. The state as a whole was a commensal system: there was no governor, all adult male citizens might freely participate in the assembly, and that body had final powers of decision within the constitution. The council consisted of persons chosen from the tribes and demes, a certain number being assigned to each, but the existing council had first to pass on the personal qualifications of all candidates with the result that no name could get on the list of approved persons unless acceptable to most major factions in the state. In any case, actions by the council could be rescinded by the assembly and the assembly could initiate actions at its own discretion.

BALANCED SOCIETIES

Three literate societies were balanced, the governor having to share with independent constituent bodies the making of policy at the center of the state. All of these societies had a patrilineal rule of descent. None had a communal economy.

1). *Iran:* The Sassanian kingdom in Iran was a heterogeneous primitive empire. Its king appointed the heads of the four provinces established for military administration and chose his own councillors and the high priest of the state church. The king was also supreme judge, commander in chief of the armed forces, and the supreme authority in the conduct of foreign relations. But he shared the central and local administration of the state with persons holding their offices independent of him. In the central bureaucracy, certain important functions were performed by hereditary right by the heads of the seven greatest noble families of the kingdom, the Sons of the Clans: superintendence of military affairs, surveillance of civil affairs, arbitration of quarrels among the nobility, command of the cavalry, collection of taxes, supervision of the royal treasuries, and care for armament and other military equipment. Although these central positions did not include the highest offices in government — for example the offices of prime minister or of chief military commander under the king — they were places of importance and honor, and the families holding them were supported in their exercise of authority by vast private revenues from their fiefs and by the force of the large numbers of their personal dependents.

Beneath the king's provincial governors were heads of villages these being men of the lesser nobility who gained office as an hereditary right. Little is known of their powers, but it is established that they served to gather taxes for the central state.

The state church in Iran was a redoubtable force. In earlier times there had been among the Medes a special tribe, not unlike the Levites in Israel or the Brahmans in India, who had priesthood as their hereditary function. When Zoroastrianism became the established faith in Iran, these ancient priestly families, the magi, served as its spiritual chiefs. The king might appoint the head of the state church, but all its priests served by right of hereditary membership in the magi and in their hands were important secular powers, some of ancient origin and some newly acquired from the state. The magi had authority to legalize births and marriages. They served as judges in most legal disputes and had power to implement their decisions. To support these activities they were granted large holdings in land and great revenues, and, within their territories, lived in accordance with laws of their own making. In their hands alone were decisions in questions of dogma and theological theory and in questions of church polity. In sum, the church had all but one of the characteristics of a religious institution fully differentiated in its society: the characteristic it lacked was recruitment of clergy and members without formal reference to kinship or other institutions.

A cautionary note: Although the weight of scholarly opinion favors my interpretation concerning the important hereditary role of the Sons of Clans at the center of the state — and hence the coding of Sassanian Iran as a balanced state — there are authorities who see that role as honorific only. Were the latter view correct, Iran should be coded unitary centralist: a code also consistent with its having a patrilineal rule of descent.

2). *Korea:* At the beginning of his dynasty, the first Yi king in Korea burned all existing land registers and began a redistribution of land aimed at the creation of a strong, centralized, bureaucratic power. Land was given to supporters and officials of the state, but only those tracts assigned to the few most notable men were made hereditary and almost all land was taxable. An examination system patterned on the Chinese was the chief road to high official position. The country was divided, as it had been in earlier times, into districts or counties. Officials of the central government were appointed to administer these units.

The central government itself was organized into a State Council, Royal Secretariat, and six ministries. As in China, there were Boards of Censors, the first of these being designed to scrutinize and criticize government policy and the action of officials, the second to do the same for actions of the king himself. There was also an Office of the Royal Lectures, ostensibly providing the king with lectures on Confucian texts, but soon evolving into a continuing forum for general debate and for the criticism both of high policy and of the behavior of the king and his officials. The staff of this Office consisted of high bureaucrats and of members of the censoring organs.

The structure of the state during the Yi period was not constant. In the first century of the dynasty, unitary centralism was the predominant pattern. But this system only masked the continuing existence of centrifugal tendencies and powers among factions of the nobility and their increasing presence within the bureaucracy. It was the bureaucratic factions, linked in important measure to regional powers, that first broke in upon the unitary structure, accomplishing this primarily through control of the censoring organs.

Unlike their relatively modest role in China, the censoring bodies in Korea came to be controlled by bureaucratic and regional factions and these factions used them to drive from government the men and policies they opposed, even including the policies of the sovereign himself. These censoring bodies reached their highest level of power in the late 15th century and in the 16th century and, as a result, the state took on a balanced structure. Reischauer and Fairbank (1958:440-42) give this picture of what followed:

> ... the censoring organs were acknowledged to be ... of pivotal importance in government. Indeed, these organs had become the chief weapons employed by rival power groups ... In any case, personal and family animosities were becoming more important than issues, and factional divisions were beginning to harden along almost hereditary lines.
>
> During the sixteenth century regional differences also became increasingly important in the development of bureaucratic cliques. The bulk of the lesser scholar-bureaucrats now lived on their agricultural holdings. There the more outstanding men gathered around themselves large numbers of relatives and disciples who had supported them when they were in office at the capital ... The bureaucratic factions thus came to have secure geographical bases. Instead of remaining ephemeral groupings ... they became semi-permanent.
>
> By the late seventeenth century ... the factional division had achieved a certain balance among four major groups — a balance which remained fairly constant for the remainder of the dynasty. These ... hardened into hereditary groupings which refused to intermarry and which worked out among themselves a rough apportionment of the numbers of persons who were to pass the official examinations and receive government posts.

Unitary centralism had been transformed into a balanced polity.

3). *Maya:* The third of these balanced polities, that of the Maya, seems simpler than the others, but this may be a function of our lack of knowledge. The Mayan aristocracy, a hereditary caste, monopolized all political and priestly offices.

There is some ambiguity as to which of several patterns of Mayan polity were indigenous and which were imposed by conquerors from Mexico. Current evidence suggests that the most typically indigenous pattern was as follows: Each Mayan state consisted of a town and of the countryside surrounding it, the whole being governed by an hereditary chief and a council. The chief, or batab, performed executive, judicial, and military functions. He presided over the local council and saw that houses were repaired and that agricultural work was conducted in a proper fashion. He judged criminal and civil cases; was head of the local warriors. The council, in turn, consisted of the heads of the town's wards. How they gained office is unclear, except that it was by some means other than appointment by the chief. Within their wards, the ward leaders had considerable autonomy and any one of them could exercise a veto on the chief's acts. Without his council's consent, a town chief could do nothing.

Some Mayan provinces consisted of confederations of independent towns, the confederation being governed by a council of town chiefs. These would properly be considered heterarchic or heteronomous in structure. Other provinces consisted of towns dependent upon the head of some one of their number. This prince appointed the chiefs of dependent towns. But in the government of his own community, the prince himself had to deal with the kind of council described in the paragraph above. His appointees in other towns were similarly limited. These provinces consisting of several towns under a prince appear to be balanced states, but stronger evidence might show that they were instances of simple centralism.

LIMITED CENTRALIST OR FEUDAL SOCIETIES

Three societies, those in Egypt, Japan, and Rome, seem to belong here. None had a communal economy. All had a bilateral rule of descent.

1). *Egypt:* In Egypt of the Middle Kingdom, the king ruled as a god who was upon earth. There was no codified law, impersonally conceived, to which magistrates might refer without consideration of the crown. Customary law was conceived to be the word of the pharaoh, articulated by him in conformance with cosmic principles of stability, justice, and order. The pharaoh's control and exercise of secular government was complete for the state as a whole, he appointing all of the central officials. But the provincial administration had largely fallen to hereditary local governors, these exercising an independent sovereignty over the villages in their territories. It is said that even posts in the central administration tended to become hereditary, but the evidence does not enable us to judge whether this entailed the development of an hereditary principle or merely the practice by pharaohs of appointing, when desirable, successive officials from families they had found trustworthy. On the record, the latter interpretation seems to me the more probable.

It is difficult to say whether Egypt was feudal or limited centralist. I lean to the second of these alternatives because the legitimacy of local governors' claims to a sovereignty over their villages exclusive of the crown's is not established.

2). *Japan:* The essentials of the Tokugawa polity in Japan have been extensively documented and their close resemblance to feudal polities in Europe are well established. The emperors were shunted to one side, becoming ceremonial figures. The new heads of state, the shoguns, governed directly only their own personal territories, holding through vassal nobles an indirect although generally effective control over the rest of the country. The nobles were to administer their holdings in conformity with the shogun's regulations, but had, within those constraints, wide powers of discretion. Persons residing on the nobles' land were their dependents and were not directly subject to the shogun's government. There was no national tax and no conscript army of all able-bodied males. There was no national system of courts to which a noble's dependents could appeal from their lord's jurisdiction.

3). *Rome:* The Roman Principate evolved from the earlier Republic, retaining and reorganizing many of the Republic's institutions. It is, therefore, helpful to describe the Principate by first sketching the structure of the Republic's constitution.

The foundation of the Republic's government was the citizenry of Rome, status as Roman citizens being extended in 90-89 B.C. to almost all Italians and in 30 B.C. to all of the men from provinces outside Italy who enlisted in the Roman Legions. Popular participation in the central government was made possible by two organizations: the Tribal Assembly and the Centuriate Assembly.

Each of the original Roman Tribes consisted of a local group of citizens. The vote of each tribe was determined by the vote of a majority of its members and the Tribal Assembly consisted of all members of all tribes, these voting by tribe, the Assembly's actions being taken by a majority of the tribes voting. The Centuriate Assembly consisted of citizens of military age, these voting by centuries (hundreds) with Assembly action being taken by a majority of the centuries voting. The number of votes in the Centuriate Assembly were apportioned by the number of centuries supplied by each class in the population, the classes being determined by property ownership. Since the wealthier classes fitted out a larger number of armed men, they had more votes and controlled the majority in the Centuriate Assembly.

The chief officers of the Roman state were elected by these two assemblies. The Tribal Assembly chose the quaestors, curule aediles, and military tribunes. The Centuriate Assembly chose the consuls, praetors, and censors. The powers of these officials must next be considered. (All had a one year term of office, this being not immediately renewable.)

Consuls: The two consuls were chief magistrates of state, exercising the old kingly power known as the imperium. This involved the right to take auspices or omens by which the gods declared their approval or disapproval of public acts. Either consul could veto the other's acts. Only the consuls, or other magistrates with imperium, could set the agenda of the Centuriate Assembly.

Military tribunes: Officers commanding the tribal levies, these being in turn commanded by the consuls or other magistrates.

Praetors: Magistrates in charge of civil jurisdiction, exercising the imperium in that sphere. They were conceived as junior colleagues of the consuls and could, if necessary, assume other consular functions: command an army, convene the Senate or an assembly.

Censors: Elected for a five year term to take a census of population and property, to let public contracts, and to assess property liable to property tax. By the end of the fourth century B.C. they had gained the right to revise the list of the senators. This revision involved an examination of the public and private conduct of the senators. Prior to this time, the consuls had had the right to make up the roll of the Senate.

Quaestors: All served as magistrates assisting the consuls. Two were designated as public treasurers; two were personal assistants to the consuls, accompanying them to war and serving as quartermasters for the troops.

Aediles: Concerned with the municipal administration of Rome: superintending public works, acting as market commissioners, serving as police magistrates.

Tribunes: Officers elected by the Tribal Assembly who had the right to extend protection to all who sought their aid, even against a magistrate in the exercise of his functions. Summoned the Tribal Assembly and presided over it.

The final significant agency of the Republic's government was the Roman Senate. The Senate had a fixed membership and, originally, consisted of appointees chosen by the consuls from the patrician clans. Senators held their seats for life unless guilty of grave public or private misconduct. Their function was to advise the consuls at the latters' request. They also acquired the right to sanction or veto resolutions passed by the Tribal Assembly. The Senate came to assign consuls and praetors to their spheres of duty. It supervised the governors of provinces, it directly governed Italy and those provinces where affairs were fairly stabilized, and it sat as a court of final authority. Although at all times the Senate represented the wealthier strata of Roman society, the possession of a certain quantity of property replaced the requirement of patrician status and one entered the Senate, not by appointment, but upon election to the quaestorship or a higher position among the magistrates.

The legal powers of the several holders of the title princeps show some variation, but, beginning with the first princeps, Augustus, those powers generally included the following: supreme military authority; command of provinces in which peace was not yet firmly established; all other powers of the consulship, the tribuneship, and the censorship; the right to nominate magistrates (praetors, quaestors, and aediles), and only these nominees to be considered by the assemblies; the right to approve new members suggested for the senatorial and equestrian orders.

The effect of these changes was to reconstruct a heterarchic state into a state with a governor, that governor having to work with the Senate and the assemblies. Is this limited centralism as Table 6 indicates? I doubt that my coding scheme catches the essentials of this Roman polity, but limited centralism comes closest to doing the job. Rome was not a balanced state because the princeps was absolute in his exercise of the central executive and judicial functions. It was not feudal because the princeps' authority extended in important matters to all free men. It was not unitary centralist because the princeps did not on his own authority name two or more levels of managers to operate the line organization of the state. It was not simple centralist because there was present a semi-independent level of management. These considerations leave limited centralism as the most appropriate code among those available.

More important, the Roman principate meets the formal requirements for limited centralism as stated in Figure 4:

   a. There was a governor – the princeps.
   b. He had of right important powers over all free men in the polity.
   c. He personally exercised or delegated the central executive and judicial functions of the state, appointing central bureaucratic officials to assist his administration of the "line" organization of government.
   d. Immediately below the princeps and those officials was the Senate and a range of magistrates and these had "line" administrative responsibilities and were by no means simply the creatures of the princeps. He nominated the magistrates and, as censor, could change the roll of the Senate, but the Tribal or Centuriate Assemblies had to approve his candidates for the magistrature, and magistrates went automatically to membership in the Senate upon completion of their terms, there to serve for life. The magistrates and Senators thus had a position jointly legitimated by princeps and assemblies. Magistrates, once in the Senate, had powers independent of the princeps, subject only to his being willing to take what was usually a politically difficult and disruptive step: that of removing them from the Senate's roll.

The main difference between the Roman case and that of most other limited centralist states is that the managerial level just described was organized as a single body, the Senate, and as a localized body of magistrates, those in Rome, rather than being dispersed in a series of quasi-autonomous localities.

UNITARY CENTRALIST SOCIETIES

1). *China, and South East Asia:* The societies in this group differ in many respects, but they are alike in having a governor whose controls, through two or more levels of managerial agents responsible to him, extended from the center of the state to units of local government.

In China during the Ming dynasty – and in eighteenth-century Vietnam where the style of government was largely Chinese in origin – this control was bolstered by Confucian doctrines and by the selection and management of a public bureaucracy, its members chosen because steeped in the society's traditional literature and certified by their superiors as of good personal and political character.

In Ceylon during the Kandyan period, the Sinhalese state authority was linked to a system of caste, the state having the duty to support that system by encouraging every man to perform the services traditional to his caste and to submit to his caste superiors.

The polities of Kandyan Ceylon, Burma (around 1800), Cambodia and Thailand in the eighteenth century derived in good part from Indian models. Moreover, all subscribed to Theravada Buddhism. In all of these countries the formal religious organization was separated from the state but was fostered and supervised by it. In all, the monks could be depended upon to challenge unjustified royal pretensions to Buddhahood or priestly status. In none could the monarch of right exercise religious authority over the religious. But in Ceylon, Buddhism, although separated from the state, was not clearly differentiated from other social institutions, whereas, in the other three countries, that differentiation had occurred. Although Buddhist doctrine in Ceylon, as elsewhere, made caste of no importance in an individual's attainment of Nirvana, the status of Buddhist monk in Ceylon became a monopoly of the highest caste and the priesthood became an organization embodying and practicing caste principles and an active agency in support of the established caste hierarchy. By contrast, monkhood in Burma, Cambodia, and Thailand was open to all devout males. In those three countries, schooling in the monasteries was open to all boys from about eight years of age, youngsters being expected to stay in school until initiated between ages 12 and 15. The sons from families of all strata from prince to fisherman might there enjoy equal status and experience the same stern discipline.

2). *Tibet (1900-1950 A.D.):* The Tibetan system in modern times — up to the conquest of Tibet by the Communist Chinese — was theocratic and unitary centralist. In principle, the Dalai Lama of Lhasa had absolute power. He was a living Buddha and head of both church and state. He appointed at his own discretion the members of the central government and chose for each of the 53 administrative districts the monk and the layman who directed affairs as agents of the central government. The village headmen, of whom there were several in each village, came to office through election by the villages' inhabitants. The Dalai Lama himself gained his position as a child when recognized as fulfilling the divinely appointed signs required.

3). *Java (1800 A.D.):* Java had for centuries been divided into principalities and other territories. By the early part of the nineteenth century, the Dutch had gained firm control over some parts of the island, the only important remaining power being that of the indigenous sultanates. The native rulers gained their posts through primogeniture. They had absolute power, appointing and dismissing at will all incumbents of the central government's offices. They appointed at their pleasure the chiefs of administrative districts. They could dispose of any land as they saw fit. Only in the villages was there some measure of independence, but that was only in those local affairs of little interest to the central regime. Villagers elected their own headmen.

4). *Hebrews (Solomon's kingdom):* The Hebrew kingdom under Solomon had coalesced from an earlier heteronomous state developed in the period of the Judges. In that earlier time, Israel was a federation of twelve tribes, these having no regularized common government but uniting for military and ceremonial purposes. Each tribe consisted of clans. Each clan was governed by the heads (the elders) of constituent extended families. Indeed even the government of tribes was amorphous, war leaders or other functionaries being appointed as required. Clans might or might not comply with tribal decisions. Each tribe did have its own territory inside which cultivated land was privately owned and the pasture land was held in common.

What powers the tribes had had were sharply attenuated by the gradual movement of the population into villages. The great patriarchal families dissolved and the elders of the villages became the most important figures in local government. The village elders were usually the elders of a localized clan. These clan organizations continued to function during the monarchy and survived both its fall and the period of the Babylonian Exile.

The kingdom arose under Saul, apparently as a union of clans and tribes against foreign enemies. Saul managed to defend the country by hiring mercenaries, paying them with fiefs. David, the second king, began his career as a mercenary soldier and, when he became chief of Israel's armed forces, depended in his campaigns primarily upon mercenaries rather than upon the native militia. As king he ruled separately in Israel and in Judah, having been chosen independently by the chief men of each as their ruler. After Solomon's reign, the two states were again separate polities and were so treated by foreign powers.

Solomon gained the throne upon David's appointment and upon his being anointed by the priests. The anointing made him a sacred person, but not a god, and qualified him to lead in worship and to perform specified religious rites. The king appointed and dismissed the chief priests, published ordinances concerning the Temple, and supervised their enforcement.

Solomon's kingdom has the characteristics of unitary centralism. There were no feudal relations between the king and his subordinates. The state was divided into twelve districts, the whole internal administration being under an officer appointed by the king and each district being organized under a prefect likewise appointed by the monarch. Little is known concerning local administration other than that village affairs were in the hands of the elders. The king established higher courts for the whole country, and appeals were forwarded to those courts from the local hearings by elders.

What made the whole structure different from other states of its kind was the role of law. The Israelite law had God as a party: it was a covenant between God and his people and was written. The king therefore did not enact law and he and his judges were to apply God's law. The judges were responsible in their judgments to that law and not to the king.

On the other hand, neither legal nor religious institutions were fully differentiated from other institutions of the society. The lower courts were in the hands of the hereditary elders, these gaining office by virtue of their membership in clans. A special non-localized tribe, the Levites, supplied a large part of the Hebrews' priesthood, priests coming to office by virtue of birth as Levites. It was only in the Temple at Jerusalem, that being a state sanctuary, that the priests were appointed and dismissed by the ruler.

6). *Incan Empire (Imperial period):* Turning finally to the Inca, one finds a unitary centralist state that operated a communal economy. The king had exclusive authority in all aspects of government, appointing to central, regional, and local posts whomever he chose. Under Incaic rule, every local district divided its agricultural produce into three portions. One third was set aside to support the state religion, one third to support the Inca's regime, and one third for local use, this to be drawn upon as necessary by local families.

DISCUSSION

I have been writing of parentage and descent and of socialization and social control. I want to make it clear that, although I have interpreted these phenomena as they appear in whole societies, I think of their general properties as being present in all persisting groups. It would be surprising, for example, were we not to find homologues of parentage, socialization, and social control in schools, fraternities, juvenile gangs, hospitals, athletic teams, business corporations, army units, and all other groups. It is, of course, important to study descent in the conventional sense of consanguineal kinship and to consider especially its grounding in sexual procreation and in the nurture of the members of a society. I suggest only that the great structural features of kinship appear in no way limited to what are conventionally defined as relations among kinsmen.

I have attempted here to provide evidence relevant for evaluating one interpretation of descent. It seems unwise at present to call it evidence for an explanation. In avoiding the stronger term, I want to reflect what we know, not to retract or equivocate. The interpretation of descent in this study is, in its logical form, an explanation: it offers some premises from which one can derive the appearance of a given rule of descent after the adoption in a society of a particular form of polity.[18] Data from four samples of societies exhibit correlations generally consistent with this explanation. They therefore are more than a raw empirical regularity but are clearly less than support for any attribution of causation. It is possible, for example, that an existing system of descent may, on occasion, limit the development or viability of polities to those consistent with it. On other occasions the reverse may occur. I find it more plausible to believe that changes in polity usually precede changes in descent, but this has yet to be shown.

---

[18] Readers who compare these studies of descent with my study of the Reformation (Swanson, 1967) may wonder why feudalism is combined with simple and unitary centralism to interpret the spread of Protestant doctrine whereas it is associated with limited centralism in interpreting descent. The rationale is as follows:

1. The key notion for my study of the Reformation is that of immanence and I propose that immanence refers to the embodiment of a social system in its acts.
2. In the present study, I propose that rules of descent symbolize the form of influence exercised by a social system as that form is determined by the necessity and possibility of the system's shaping in its participants of desired skills and commitments.
3. I propose that immanence is less likely to the extent that participants in an association have, by virtue of their positions in that association, formal rights to determine what acts the social system will undertake or how those acts will be implemented.

There is, moreover, a large body of information that should be reexamined before further ventures with the theory presented here. This information constitutes the heart of Murdock's classic study Social Structure (1949: Chapter 8, Appendix A.) He proposes in that book that changes in kinship occur in a particular order: the first rules to change being those governing residence; the next, rules of descent; the last of all being principles concerning kinship terminology. His rationale is necessarily complex (1949, 200-02).

---

4. It is clear, I propose, that social systems in which participants have such an independent role will not be able adequately to socialize those participants. This will obviously be the case under heteronomous, heterarchic, and balanced regimes and, under such regimes, one expects an absence of immanental doctrines in religion and the presence of a patrilineal principle in descent or, at high evolutionary levels, in theological formulae.

5. Under certain regimes men participate in their society's social system only as its agents and they also retain a formal status as elements in that system rather than status as mere parts. The clearest instances are in commensal and simple centralist regimes. Under such regimes one expects immanental doctrines in religion and, depending upon the evolutionary level attained, matrilineal emphases either in descent or in theology.

6. Under one type of regime, unitary centralism, men have a role in their social system only as its agents and as its parts. Because of their role as agents, one again expects immanental doctrines in religion. Because men are conceived to be only parts of the social system, socialization, while possible, is unnecessary; and one expects, depending upon the society's evolutionary level, a patrilineal emphasis in descent or in theology.

7. This brings us to feudalism and limited centralism. They are revealing cases for our theories because they are so similar in some respects and, on critical features, dissimilar.

Consider, first, their connection with immanence. Under both feudalism and limited centralism, a subordinate must obey the orders of his overlord. But, under feudalism, a vassal lord has no formal right to serve as his overlord's agent in the implementation of policy. The overlord may, in principle, choose whom he pleases for that purpose. Under limited centralism the situation is different. Principal subordinates of an overlord have formally the exclusive right to be his agents in implementing policies. If the overlord's policies are to be carried out, he must employ these particular subordinates for that purpose. Under feudalism, an overlord can break his ties to vassals. Under limited centralism, an overlord does not choose the principal subordinates who will implement his policies nor has he the power to dismiss them. In sum, the feudal principle gives the overlord power to select his subordinates in operating the society's social system, whereas the principle of limited centralism requires that subordinate agents of a social system be those persons who already have important and independent positions in the society's association. For these reasons, one expects an immanental religious outlook under feudalism but not under limited centralism.

Consider next the connection between these two regimes and descent. Under limited centralism, the special powers of subordinates are considerable yet their lord must be obeyed. They have discretion, formal and de facto, in the manner in which orders are obeyed, but not in whether to obey. Under feudalism, subordinates must again obey a superior's commands. Although a vassal has no right to act as his overlord's agent, and although, if called upon to do so, he must acquiesce, he has in fact considerable independent powers, himself having lands and vassals over which he has exclusive control. He may not legitimately use these independent powers to demand the right to serve as his overlord's agent nor to modify the overlord's policies when serving as his agent. Yet they exist whether or not the vassal is officially his overlord's agent, and the feudal "contract" demands that an overlord respect the rights of vassal lords over their own subordinates and agree not to undertake actions that would compromise those rights. Thus, with respect to the formulation and implementation of his overlord's policies, the vassal lord has no rights. Nonetheless he has important powers in other matters, namely over his own subordinates. The conclusion I have drawn is that under limited centralism and under feudalism, major subordinates have important independent rights in governing local affairs. In both cases, the general government is clearly under the exclusive direction of their superior. In these circumstances, socialization is necessary and, to a considerable extent, is possible, but it is not easy. Social control must be exercised as well. This led me to forecast a bilateral rule of descent in both situations.

... quite different external influences are capable of producing an identical effect upon social organization (i.e., a kinship system), and ... there are several series of multiple factors capable of producing different effects. If this is true ... the search for the sources of change must be shifted from the external factors to the social structure itself. We must look for some aspect of social organization which acts as a filter, which is capable of responding in only a limited number of ways but by each of them to a variety of quite diverse external stimuli. Such a structural feature must, in addition, be peculiarly sensitive to outside influences and at the same time be itself especially competent to effect compensatory readjustments elsewhere in the system.

... kinship terminology reacts very slightly if at all to external influences ... Rules of descent and the kin groups resulting therefrom are also relatively immune to forces from outside the social organization ...

The one aspect of social structure that is peculiarly vulnerable to external influences is the rule of residence ...

It is in respect to residence that changes in economy, technology, property, government, or religion first alter the structural relationships of related individuals to one another, giving an impetus to subsequent modifications in forms of the family, in consanguineal and compromise kin groups, and in kinship terminology.

By this line of reasoning, inconsistencies among the principles of a kinship system are explained as the failure of descent or terminology to adjust to prior changes in residence.[19] If changes in rules of descent are usually produced by new political developments, those developments should, by Murdock's argument, first produce changes in rules of residence.

An inspection of Tables 7 and 8 shows relationships consistent with that argument. Rules of residence and of descent in sixty non-literate societies (those tabulated in Table 4) are closely associated with one another and are highly correlated, both individually and in combination, with these societies' regimes. But these relationships are also consistent with widely different sequences of change among residence, descent, and regime. The causal connection I have postulated between changes in regime and subsequent changes in descent is only one of these. If that connection is explored through further research, it will be important to consider the other sequences, beginning with Murdock's own seminal proposals.

---

[19]Professor Melvin Ember has begun work on conditions related to the rule of residence employed in primitive societies, and has reported an important first finding: "... when warfare is continual and males predominate in the division of labor, residence is significantly likely to be patrilocal; and when warfare is continual and females predominate in the division of labor, residence is likely to be matrilocal. But in the absence of continual warfare there was no relationship between division of labor and residence." (see Ember and Baldwin, n.d.). Given some independence between rules governing descent and those governing residence, it would not be surprising if they proved to originate in different conditions. It may be, however, that, among the simpler primitives, it is simple centralism and commensalism, both related to matriliny, that have an advantage for the sustained conduct of warfare over heterarchy and heteronomy, the latter related to patriliny. Were this so, the rule of residence might follow primarily from a society's regime when taken together with the role of women in the society's economy.

TABLE 7
REGIME, DESCENT, AND RESIDENCE

Descent	Residence*	Regime**												
		Heteronomous		Commensal			Heterarchic	f	g	h	i	j	Uncodeable	Total
		a	b	c	d	e								
Patrilineal	A	5	2	1	1	.	4	3	1	.	.	2	1	20
	B	2	.	.	.	.	.	1	.	.	.	.	.	3
	C	.	.	.	.	.	.	.	.	.	.	1	.	1
	D	.	.	.	.	.	.	.	.	.	.	.	.	0
Matrilineal	A	.	.	.	.	.	.	.	.	.	.	.	.	0
	B	.	.	.	.	.	.	.	.	.	.	.	.	0
	C	.	.	.	.	.	.	.	1	.	1	.	.	2
	D	.	.	4	.	.	1	.	2	1	3	.	1	12
Bilateral	A	.	.	.	.	1	.	.	1	1	.	.	.	3
	B	.	5	.	2	.	.	.	1	.	.	.	1	9
	C	.	1	1	3	.	.	.	.	.	1	.	.	6
	D	.	.	2	2	.	.	.	.	.	.	.	.	4
Total		7	8	8	8	1	5	4	6	2	5	3	3	60

* The codes under residence are combinations of those employed in the journal *Ethnology* which regularly presents classifications of the characteristics of the simpler societies. A-patrilocal; B-virilocal (without localized unilineal kin groups) ; C-ambilocal, bilocal, or utrolocal (optionally with or near either parents); or ambilocal with option between patrilocal (or virilocal) and avunculocal; or neolocal; D-matrilocal; or avunculocal (with or near maternal uncle); or uxorilocal (without matrilocal and matrilineal kin groups); or ambilocal with option between uxorilocal and avunculocal.

** The lower-case letters for Regime refer to the following classifications: *a*-individuated heteronomous; *b*-commensal heteronomous; *c*-commensal; *d*-commensal with communal economy; *e*-commensal with differentiated religion; *f*-balanced; *g*-limited centralist; *h*-feudal; *i*-simple centralist; *j*-unitary centralist.

TABLE 8
REGIME, DESCENT, AND RESIDENCE
(Compiled from Table 7)

Descent	Residence	Regime		
		Individuated heteronomous, Heterarchic, Balanced, and Unitary centralist.	Commensal, and Simple centralist.	Commensal Heteronomous, Commensal with communal Economy, Limited Centralist, Feudal and Differentiated Religion
Patrilineal	A	14	1	4
	B	3	0	0
	C	1	0	0
	D	0	0	0
Matrilineal	A	0	0	0
	B	0	0	0
	C	0	1	1
	D	1	7	3
Bilateral	A	0	0	3
	B	0	0	8
	C	0	2	4
	D	0	2	2
Total		19	13	25

To this point I have sketched Murdock's proposals in simplified form. His actual ideas are more qualified, his argument more probabilistic. For example, he pictures rules of residence as relevant for one type of kin group and rules of descent as relevant for a different type. These groups exist simultaneously in the same population and have some overlap of membership. "... the form of a residential kin group is determined primarily by the prevailing rule of residence, that of a consanguineal kin group primarily by the rule of descent." (1949:42). Thus the nuclear family is almost always a residential kin group, but its members are linked by descent to a wider group of kinsmen. In some societies the widest residential group, perhaps a clan, is coterminous with the widest consanguineal kin group. In many societies this is not so. The very existence in every society of two types of kin group and the fact that they are only sometimes coterminous makes it more plausible that they may respond directly but to different governing conditions outside the kinship system. Were this the case, and should a population thereby develop a rule of descent somewhat inconsistent with its rule of residence, some organizational mechanism would be required to adjust relations between residential and consanguineal kin groups.

Working with historical information about primitive peoples, Murdock finds many instances in which changes in residence were followed by consistent changes in descent. He also finds many cases in which no such change in descent occurred. He does not seem to find cases in which changes in descent or kinship terminology appeared first, these followed by consistent changes in residence. Other investigators might interpret these same records differently.

Let us suppose, however, that they agreed with Murdock's essential findings. What would his historical observations suggest about the validity of my proposal that certain political changes produce changes in descent? It is hard to say because Murdock attaches further complex qualifications to his basic propositions. He says, for example, that his scheme applies only to "the normal order of change among the principal elements of social organization" and to "any social system which has attained a comparatively stable equilibrium" and which then "begins to undergo change" (Murdock, 1949: 221-22). He also adds such important qualifications as these (Murdock, 1949: 208-210):

> A new rule of residence once established what are its effects? In the first place, it begins to exert an influence on kinship terminology . . . Since, however, the relative efficacy of residence rules is not especially high, the expected changes in kinship nomenclature frequently do not appear until after the establishment of a new rule of descent. It is with respect to unilinear groupings of kinsmen that rules of residence exert their most important influence . . .
>
> A change to neolocal residence from any form of unilocal residence - matrilocal, patrilocal, or avunculocal - has a disruptive effect upon existing unilinear groupings. Clans are especially susceptible. . . . Unilocal extended families break up nearly as readily . . . Lineages, sibs, and moieties are more resistant, and if functionally important may survive for a considerable time. They . . . tend eventually to disappear entirely . . .
>
> While neolocal and bilocal residence invariably result ultimately in the loss of unilinear descent, and appear to be the only means by which such loss can ordinarily occur, the adoption of unilocal residence in a bilateral society, though it favors the development of a corresponding unilinear rule of descent, by no means produces such a rule inevitably . . .
>
> Unilocal residence does not produce lineages or sibs directly . . . What matrilocal or patrilocal residence accomplishes is to assemble in spatial proximity to one another a group of unilinearly related kinsmen of the same sex, together with their spouses. Local conditions may or may not favor the development of the particular kinds of social bonds between the members of such a group that would constitute them into an extended family or localized kin group. If such bonds are formed, and extended families or other residential kin groups make their appearance, the society is exceedingly likely to develop unilinear descent in due time . . .

DISCUSSION

If these many qualifications make it impossible sharply to compare his theory and findings with mine, his work nonetheless forces us to consider the possibility that both approaches are in some sense correct and it encourages us to consider interpretations that would be compatible with both. Here are examples of such interpretations:

1). A change to neolocal residence will inevitably force the development of a bilateral rule of descent, but such a change will occur only after there has appeared a form of polity congenial to bilaterality. On the other hand, a form of unilocal residence can be adopted in a society without regard to the form of polity then existing.

2). The forces producing rules of descent are different from those producing rules of residence, but the two happen often to be systematically linked and, as a result, these two sets of rules are "consistent" with one another. For various reasons, this systematic linkage is not present in something from a fourth to a third of known societies, hence their rules of descent and residence are discrepant.[20]

3). Whatever else may be true, a discrepancy in rules governing kinship will in some manner generate forces toward establishing consistency among those rules, it being most frequent that the factors determining rules of residence are more potent among these forces than are factors producing rules of descent.

4). Factors producing systems of residence are different from those producing rules of descent, the former being more labile. On the other hand, no system of residence can be established that would preclude the subsequent establishment of a principle of descent consistent with the slower-acting forces that govern descent.

Obviously these are only a few of the possible suggestions. They do indicate that Murdock's work poses important questions for mine but that our two studies may not be inconsistent.

There remain for brief consideration two further points. The first concerns the relation between my findings and the evolution of societies, evolution understood as what Sahlins and Service call "general cultural evolution: . . . passage from less to greater energy transformation, lower to higher levels of integration, and less to greater all-round adaptability."[21] Even casual scanning shows the main points: in the societies considered here, lineality varies according to regime and not according to a society's evolutionary status; of these societies, some of the simplest (e.g., those in which the extended or joint family is coterminous with the society) and the most advanced (those in which polity and religion are institutionally differentiated from one another and from other institutions) have in common certain basic political characteristics and a bilateral rule of descent; there is no doubt that some matrilineal societies (e.g., those formed as simple centralist states) are organizationally more advanced than some patrilineal societies (e.g., the simpler heterarchies); there are patrilineal societies at a higher evolu-

---

[20] This proportion is purely speculative. It was estimated from Murdock (1949:59).
[21] Sahlins and Service, eds., (1960:30). See also Parsons, (1966:1-29).

tionary level (most of those having unitary centralism) than is any matrilineal society.[22]

The second and final point: I have proposed that a rule of descent always symbolizes the relations of parentage between a society and its "children." In the simpler societies, the form taken by the political system usually provides a good index of the form of descent that will be present. In the more advanced societies, however, the rule of descent reflects the relations of a society's members with a social order in which a religious and political structure are integrated with one another while being also sharply differentiated. These advanced societies all have a bilateral rule of descent. Nonetheless they differ in the form taken by their political regimes. I have shown elsewhere (Swanson, 1967, 1968) that a typology of regimes like the one employed in the present study will account for the distribution among the advanced societies in Reformation Europe of Calvinism, Lutheranism, and Catholicism and have interpreted the differences among these religious standpoints as reflecting the kinds of difference in style of parentage described in the present account. Thus it seems that the bilateral rule of

---

[22] a) It may be of significance in interpreting contemporary as well as primitive societies that the data suggest a species of equivalence between a communal economy and a differentiated religion.

b) It might be thought that age-societies, serve, when present, to integrate special interests with common interests and, hence, that they should be linked to bilaterality. This might be implied by the theoretical treatment given those societies in S.N. Eisenstadt's well-known monograph (Eisenstadt, 1955). Eisenstadt describes six types of age-society. Twenty-seven of the 40 primitive societies he describes are among those in the World Ethnographic Sample, hence can quickly be examined for rule of descent: The main finding is that societies with a patrilineal rule of descent appear more often among those sampled by Eisenstadt than in the World Ethnographic Sample, the respective percentages being 70 and 44. I notice, moreover, that the considerable majority of Eisenstadt's cases are heterarchic, heteronomous, or balanced states. May it be that, contrary to his suggestion that age-societies arise to mediate strains produced by individuals' conflicting loyalties to kin and to extra-kin economic units, those societies sometimes or often arise to link men otherwise divided into the special interest groups that are accepted as legitimate in their polity?

c) This point in our discussion is also a convenient place to note that matrilineal societies are less likely to have complex polities. Thus, in the World Ethnographic Sample, Murdock codes 10 per cent of the matrilineal societies as "little states" and 5 per cent as full-fledged "states." The comparative percentages for patrilineal societies are 13 per cent and 15 per cent; for bilateral societies, 4 per cent and 18 per cent. Are the most complex matrilineal polities feudal in form, or unitary or limited centralist, or balanced?

The four full-fledged matrilineal "states" coded by Murdock are the Bemba, Fur, Nayar, and Wolof. Two of these, the Bemba and Wolof, had simple centralist polities. The Bemba king appointed the district chiefs who in turn appointed the village headmen. The Wolof ruler named chiefs, each in charge of a group of villages. It appears that these, in turn, named the village headmen or, alternatively, that the headmanship was hereditary. Consult: Richards (in Fortes and Evans-Pritchard, 1940); and Gamble (1957:55-61).

The other two cases cannot be coded from information I have examined. Although the sources agree that the chain of command among the Fur extended from sultan to chiefs to sub-chiefs to village headmen, they differ concerning accession to these offices. Felkin (1885) states that all these positions were hereditary. Beaton tells us (1948) that accession followed a "strong hereditary principle," which is not the same thing. The other sources are less specific. Consult: Lampen (1950) and Arkell, (1951a, b). Gough tells us that the Nayar kingdoms had kings, district chiefs, and village headmen (and royal feudatories placed between the king and the chiefs) but provides no data on accession to office. See Gough, (in Schneider and Gough, 1962a, b).

descent common to all of these European societies reflects the relations of parentage implied by the basic institutional arrangements found in all societies at this evolutionary level and that the differences in religious doctrine reflect the variations upon that style of parentage that different forms of regime can generate. These further results document the point with which I began this discussion: the principles and forms of parentage transcend what are conventionally defined as consanguineal relations among kinsmen.

APPENDIX I

CODING PROCEDURES

I. OBJECTIVE

To explore and characterize the relations between a society's association and its social system.

The method is the identification of all levels of decision-making in a population from the individual up through the total society and the characterization of each level's composition, powers, internal organization, and interrelations with other levels. Given the objective, the interrelations are of greatest importance, other information being needed to specify those interrelations.

Information is sought about indigenous structures for making decisions. Unless otherwise specified, consider as your problem the structure of the last available indigenous government.

An author's factual observations should be preferred over his interpretations.

II. DEFINITIONS

A. The Total Society

Consider a society to be like any other group: an organization that makes decisions and implements them. A society is that organization in a population having original, independent, and ultimate jurisdiction. Note: it may not be a strong organization, but it exists, it functions, and it is expected to go on doing so.

1. The group or its representatives must meet at least once a year. Organizations will be counted as meeting this criterion if there is an effective obligation among participants to join together for common and customary action under stated circumstances (such as common defense or sharing of food in time of disaster or for acts of retribution). Always consider a governor and his advisers as "representatives."

2. It must have customary procedures for making decisions, such as rules for taking a vote or sounding out opinions: acknowledged roles, whether formal, which participants hold in decision making (e.g., representative, officer, voter, audience, nonofficial participant, member, constituent, consultant). Alternatively, there may not be visible procedures for making decisions, but there are customary ties that link or retain people for joint activity as needed.

3. The group must be considered legitimate by its members. This means that the members must approve of the group's existence, its goals, and its procedure of operation. They may or may not agree with all aspects of the group's organization, but there must not be evidence that they challenge the desirability or justice of its existence or its general purposes and procedures.
4. There must not be evidence which suggests that the group is perceived by its members as failing to persist into the indefinite future.
5. The group must have three or more members.
6. It must make decisions on actions which have a significant effect on its members (e.g., war and peace, the punishment of crimes, the distribution of food, the allocation of the more important means for producing sustenance, the formation of alliances with other groups, the allocation of "civic" duties such as taxes, conscription for military service or for labor service).
7. It must not be an agency of another organization. This usually eliminates such organizations as armed services, magical and religious organizations, groups of slaves, specialized divisions of a government, specialized divisions of an economy such as the organization that operates a market or cultivates crops or tends the herds, and educational or socializing organizations such as schools and organized age-sets.
8. It must be viewed as a distinctive organization by its members over whom it has jurisdiction.
9. Note that the nuclear family may be the only organization in a population that meets the preceding criteria. A nuclear family is any group consisting of the partners to a marriage and the children of their union. A polygamous family is counted as a single nuclear family.

B. Constituent Bodies and Governors

The objective in defining constituent bodies is to delimit the body politic: persons and/or groups having such full political rights in a society as are available to anyone other than a governor. These bodies call our attention to that part of the population from which parties may legitimately come who, with or without a governor, have some role in the exercise of gubernaculum.

The specifications for constituent bodies given here were developed from a study of medieval Europe. They may not do for some primitive societies. On the other hand, almost all societies have a body politic. The problem is to learn how to specify it objectively. One should not be deceived by some statements about some primitive rulers: e.g., that they own all the land or that all members of the society are possessions of the ruler. An inspection of the data for societies about which such statements are made often shows that individuals or groups have some rights: e.g., the right to use land, the right to a customary trial, the right to the produce from land they work. Remember also that almost all societies have some concept like that of "eminent domain": the right of government to take possession of private holdings for a public purpose (usually with compensation to the private owner). And in almost all societies there is some sense in which government "possesses" the physical bodies of the citizen: the right to use them for a public purpose as conscript laborers or as tax payers or as soldiers. Such rights of eminent domain or of possession of citizens do not of themselves result in the citizens' lack of full membership in the society or their enslavement.

In any case, describe whatever the data show, and it may be that there are no constituent bodies in a given society.

1. Constituent Bodies

Constituent bodies are all parties (individuals and groups) in a society's adult population who are recognized as its members and as free. They do not include parties who are members of a society but unfree or free inhabitants who are not members. Among medieval European societies we find some in which many inhabitants had only limited freedom but nonetheless were defined as members of the society. They were liable, for example, for taxes and for military service. This was the position of landless peasants in Denmark, Prussia, and Hungary. We also find societies, typically smaller ones, having more free permanent inhabitants than members. This situation arose in several of the Swiss cantons, and in each the distinction between the rights of mere inhabitants and those of citizens was sharpened in favor of the latter.

Constituent bodies are all parties having certain civil and political rights, providing, of course, that these rights are available to any adults in a society's population: the right to own land and/or business enterprises; the right of access to the central government's courts for the adjudication of civil, political, or criminal actions brought under laws administered at least in part by the central government; the right to protection by the central government against foreign powers; the right of participation in whatever procedures exist for exercising jurisdictio. (Jurisdictio is defined below under V. G.) Groups or individuals may be constituent bodies.

2. Governor

Some societies are headed by a governor. An example would be medieval English society under its king. Other societies, like those in medieval Venice or Zurich, lacked a governor. A governor may be an individual or a group. In either case, a governor is organizationally separated from the body politic (i.e., the aggregate of constituent bodies) and from agencies through which the body politic may exercise jurisdictio, for example, from legislatures. A governor has independent rights in the exercise of gubernaculum. (Gubernaculum is defined below under V F.)

To be organizationally separate from the body politic and from a legislature, an agency must have six characteristics:

a. Term of office: A governor may come to office by one of many routes. He may come by inheritance or by the choice of his predecessor. He may be chosen by a legislature. He may be selected by the entire body politic. Whatever the route by which a governor comes to his post, he must obtain the right to a term in office exceeding two years. The point of this minimal requirement is to insure that the governor not be too immediately dependent on the wishes of some constituency.

b. Tenure in office: A governor must have the security in office provided by a stated term and by the rule that he can be removed from office, if at all, only if he violates such conditions of office as are established when he accepts it and if that violation is determined by due process, that is, by some judicial procedure which protects the governor's stated prerogatives as well as prerogatives of persons who challenge his continued right to office.

c. Confidentiality of procedures: The incumbent must not be legally obliged to provide any other person or any official body with such information as it may desire concerning the procedures by which he and subordinates exercise his rights, nor may he legally be called upon to do so upon the completion of his term of office.

d. Guaranteed support: There must be some guarantee prior to his taking office that resources needed for the discharge of his responsibilities will be supplied him. These may take any appropriate form: income from a crown's hereditary lands, feudal dues or services, taxes and aids, fealty of kinsmen.

e. Separation from the body politic: If the governor is a group, it does not consist of more than 10 per cent of the members of the body politic.

f. Separation from agencies specifically those of the body politic: The governor must not be an agency through which the body politic exercises jurisdictio.

A governor has independent rights in the exercise of gubernaculum. These include:

a. Scope of initiative: A governor has all aspects of gubernaculum within his purview and may take the first steps toward action with respect to any or all of them.

b. Administrative independence: A governor has sole authority to administer at least some of the significant policies that guide the exercise of gubernaculum. He may, for example, have the decisive word in determining how a system of provincial courts shall be organized or how policies regarding foreign trade shall be implemented or how a newly created army shall be trained.

c. Executive authority: No one has the right to disobey a governor's decision except by authority of established judicial procedures which protect the governor's rights as well as those of complainants.

By these three criteria, every head of government is not a governor. The dukes (doges) of Venice, like the kings of modern England, reigned but did not rule. Many leaders of primitive societies are merely spokesmen for the body politic, articulating its point of view. By these same criteria, a governor need not have exclusive competence over gubernaculum. A king or self-perpetuating oligarchy may, for example, be forced to exercise gubernaculum in some matters with the consent of a council, that council consisting of representatives of a legislature and responsible to it. But the existence of this council need not infringe on the organizational separation of the governor's other powers from the legislature's or on the independence of his rights in gubernaculum.

III. CODE: SOCIETY

A. What organization in this population best meets the foregoing criteria for a total society?
B. State exactly how its structure meets criteria 1, 2, 5, and 6.
C. What organization would be the next best choice as a definition of the total society in this population?*

*Definitions of organizations:

Territorial organizations

0. Household, hamlet, scattered rural neighborhood, small nomadic band. There are no villages, towns, or cities.
1. Village. A residential unit or encampment with at least 50 people and/or there is a kraal, compound, village, or encampment especially designated as that of chief or king. There are no towns or cities.
2. District, sector — any political organization which unifies two or more units coded as 0 or 1 above and which is not codable as 3, 4, or 5.
3. Town, city. A town is a residential unit of 300 to 1,999 people. A city is a residential unit with a population of 2,000 or more.
4. Chiefdom — any political organization with a chief executive which unifies two or more units coded as 0, 1, or 3 above.
5. Kingdom — any political organization with a chief executive which unifies two or more chiefdoms.
6. Intertribal league — any political organization which unites two or more

tribes but is not codable as a kingdom. For a definition of tribe, see Code 7 below.

Y. No purely territorial organization. (i.e., organization is based on principles of kinship).

Kinship organizations (preferred over territorial organizations)

0. Household – nuclear family.
1. Extended family – two or more nuclear families united by consanguineal bonds such as those between parent and child or between two siblings.
2. Lineage – a consanguineal kin group produced by a rule of unilinear descent when it includes only persons who can actually trace their common relationship through a specific series of remembered genealogical links in the prevailing line of descent.
3. Gens – a patrilineal sib. A sib is a consanguineal kin group acknowledging a traditional bond of common descent but unable always to trace the actual genealogical connections between individuals.
4. Kindred – a bilateral kin group of near kinsmen who participate together in important ceremonial occasions involving relatives and who are expected to support one another against outsiders. It is never the same for any two persons except siblings.
5. Clan – meets three specifications: (a) it is based explicitly on a unilinear rule of descent which unites its central core members, (b) it has residential unity, and (c) it exhibits actual social integration – i.e., positive group sentiment and a recognition of inmarrying spouses as an integral part of membership.
6. Phratry – two or more sibs who recognize a purely conventional unilinear bond of kinship.
7. Tribe or kin-based union of tribes – a political union of two or more sibs, clans, phratries, or moieties (a moiety being one of a dichotomous pair of sibs or phratries), (or a political union of two or more extended families which is not otherwise classifiable as a territorial or kinship organization) providing that each of the groups in question is exogamous within itself and endogamous within the union, and providing that representatives of these exogamous kinship groups comprise the government of their union.

IV. DESCRIPTIVE SKETCH

List and briefly describe all levels of decision-making (e.g., government) between the total society and its individual members. Indicate for each:

APPENDIX I

1. Is this level a creation of levels above it? Did it create them? Describe.
2. Does it develop policies of its own? Describe.
3. Does it implement policies developed at higher levels? Describe.
4. How do its "officials" obtain their position? Lose them?
5. How is the level organized internally for making and implementing decisions?
6. Describe any control exercised over this level by others or by it over them and not otherwise covered in these questions.

V. CODE: SOCIETY'S REGIME

                      Code 9: none observed
                      Code 10: other (specify)

A. Scope of regime's authority
  1. All free men
  2. Governments of constituent bodies, those having autonomous powers within their several domains to determine one or more of the following:
     a. The judicial structure and procedures employed
     b. The taxes that are levied and the units which pay them
     c. The laws and ordinances that may be published and enforced
B. Authorities having independent and original jurisdiction over some aspects of the regime's central exercise of gubernaculum (governors are indicated by an asterisk)
  1. Assembly of all members of the body politic
  2. A group of kinsmen
  3. A Diet (that is, one or more houses of Estates)
  4. One or more councils
  5. An individual
C. Agencies by which constituent bodies share in the regime's central exercise of gubernaculum
  1. Assembly of all members of the body politic
  2. Diet
  3. One or more councils or committees
  4. Agencies are one or more of authorities specified under B above

D. Constituent bodies sharing in the regime's central exercise of gubernaculum by means of the agencies specified in C above:
  1. All members of the body politic
  2. Towns
  3. Rural districts – all free inhabitants and/or all landowners
  4. Local organizations of nobles and/or gentry

5. Greater noble families
6. Guilds
7. Administrative units (for example, quarters, amts) other than the above

E. Constituent bodies sharing in the regime's local exercise of gubernaculum (the agencies by means of which this power is exercised being the constituent bodies themselves or one of those listed under C above)
   10. There seem not to be any such local jurisdictions to be exercised

F. Powers of constituent bodies sharing in the regime's central exercise of gubernaculum
   1. Maintaining the regime
      a. Elect governor
      b. Share in exercise of regencies
      c. Right as an assemblage of constituent bodies to rebel against governor who breaches their privileges
      d. Right as individual constituent bodies to rebel against governor who breaches their privileges
   2. Control over administrative staffing
      a. Name some or all major officials, these then being responsible in some measure to the constituent bodies
      b. Remove major officials who breach the law
      c. Name some or all major officials
      d. Nominate a slate of candidates for some or all major official posts, governor making appointments from this slate
      e. Consent to the accession to office of major officials named by governor
   3. Supervision of administrative operations
      a. Supervise the collection and/or expenditure of taxes and aids
      b. Supervise trade and commerce
      c. Establish and/or maintain armies, militia, or fortifications
      d. Determine the uses made of armies or militia
      e. Consent to the establishing or revocation of alliances
      (Constituent bodies listed under A or C above)
   7. Select or comprise authorities having independent and original jurisdiction in regime

G. Powers of constituent bodies sharing in the regime's central exercise of jurisdictio
   1. Organization to exercise these powers:
      a. Established rights of participation
      b. Established rules of procedure in deliberative sessions
      c. Established dates for meetings or right of participants to convene ses-

APPENDIX I 73

   sions as desired
   d. Established apparatus to pursue the legislature's work when that body is not in session
2. Decisions for which consent of constituent bodies may be sought (if their consent is required in principle, type of decision involved is followed by a cross-hatch [#].)
   a. Make or change laws
   b. Codify laws
   c. Exercise of highest judicial functions (for example, decisions in cases of treason, rebellion, lese-majesty)
   d. Declare war or conclude treaties of peace
   e. Levy or renew taxes; obtain or make loans
7. Constituent bodies listed under B above also undertake the regime's central exercise of jurisdictio

H. Powers of constituent bodies sharing in the regime's local* exercise of gubernaculum
   1. Control over staffing of local units of national administrative structure
      a. Name some or all major local officials, these then being responsible in some measure to the constituent bodies
      b. Name some or all major local officials
      c. Consent to major local officials named by governor
      d. Nominate a slate of candidates for major local official posts, governor making appointments from this slate
      e. Governor must choose major local officials from among that locality's inhabitants
   2. Control over operation of local units of national administrative structure
      a. Control all or a large share of the local administration of the national system of justice and general administration
      b. Right to subject local administration by national officials to judicial review

   10. There seem not to be any local jurisdictions to be exercised
I. By way of review:
   If there is a governor:
   1. Does the governor designate the persons who, at two or more operating levels in the polity (e.g., central bureaucracy, regions, provinces, villages),

---

*Sometimes a population is divided into administrative units (e.g., guilds) that are not localized geographically. Consider those administrative subdivisions as meeting the requirement of "localization."

direct administrative and/or judicial activities at lower levels?
   a. No.
   b. Yes.
2. Is there some operating level of administration and/or justice intermediate between the lowest level and the highest over which persons or groups have rights and powers independent of the governor's?
   a. No.
   b. Yes.
3. Do the governor's rights and powers extend in some or all important matters of administration and/or justice to all free men? (In some societies "all free men" will mean families, villages, or other groups, they, and not separate individuals, having political rights.)
   a. No.
   b. Yes.

VI. SOME MODELS

Here are several models of government. The case you are now coding may not fit any one of them, but it comes closer to one than to the others. Which model is closest? What discrepancies exist between that model and the case being coded? When in serious doubt as to which of two codes from the following list to use, use the one that comes first: A-4, A-2, B, A-3, A-1.

In all of the models from A-1 through A-4, there is a central governor over all free men. The models differ in the scope of his powers and in the extent to which he shares them.

Model A-1: The governor has, in principle, direct control over all free men. The governor formulates certain policies by his own authority. Intermediate subdivisions of the body politic (i.e., those between the central state and smallest units of local government) are at once required to implement those policies and empowered to act as the governor's agents in supervising that implementation. The governor may legitimately appoint, approve, or dismiss the officials at these intermediate levels.

The governor's policies apply uniformly to all units at any given level of decision-making. Although the governor may find it expedient or convenient to select councillors or the agents who implement his policies from some particular part of the population (e.g., other members of his clan, merchants, nobles) there is no formal limitation on his right to choose, appoint, or dismiss his councillors and agents solely at his own discretion. Neither the governor, nor persons chosen

APPENDIX I

by him, may legitimately appoint, approve, or dismiss the formal leaders of the smallest units of local government, nor does the central state create most such units. (Describe)

Model A-2: Identical with Model A-1 except: The governor's power to choose, appoint, or dismiss persons who implement his policies at the intermediate level is subject to some important limitations, these having the effect of giving intermediate areas a significant voice in that implementation. For example, the intermediate areas (districts, villages, etc.) may choose these local agents, the governor may have to choose his agents from among local inhabitants or from a list of nominees prepared by the locality, the locality may have to agree to an agent of the governor's before that agent can assume office or may have recourse to the courts or other formal procedures through which an undesired agent can be removed. (Describe what is involved.)

Model A-3 Identical with Model A-1 with the further proviso that the central administrative system has created or approved the creation of the smallest units of government (e.g., villages, hamlets, five-family neighborhoods) in this society. Or: Although the smallest units of government were not created or authorized by the central administrative system, that system has the power to appoint or dismiss the formal leaders of those units.

Model A-4: The governor has, in principle, direct control over all free men or over the subdivisions described in Model B. This model differs from Model B and from all other Models under A in one critical respect: The governor is formally required to share his central exercise of gubernaculum with constituent bodies or their representatives or the units under the governor constitute a shifting confederation of local groups, these united largely by convenience or expediency.

Model B: Subdivisions of the body politic have in their own right original jurisdiction over their subordinates, the governor having the right of dealing directly only with those subdivisions, not their subordinates.

Subordinates of subdivisions of the body politic are that subdivision's vassals, citizens, property, etc., but not the governor's.

The governor's policies apply to subdivisions of the body politic only as a consequence of the governor's separate negotiations with each. There is, thus, the possibility of variations in the application of those policies among units at any given level of decision-making.

Model C: The entire body politic, either directly, or in part through officials chosen by that body politic and answerable to it, deals with all matters under gubernaculum. It performs all functions of a governor and exercises all rights of jurisdictio.**

Model D: Persons come to exercise powers of gubernaculum or jurisdictio only as representatives of their personal interests or of specific groups in the body politic.**

It is not the case that:

a. Persons representative of the society as a whole must approve candidates nominated by constituent bodies before they can be considered acceptable as participants in gubernaculum.
b. Decisions are commonly possible only if supported by all or the large majority of representatives of constituent bodies (i.e., two-thirds or more).
c. Participants in gubernaculum are chosen by the drawing of lots from a list of all members of the body politic.

Model E: Direct democracy in a simple society. There is only one level of decision-making above individuals and/or households. Adult citizens or the older men meet as needed to decide important matters, at least some of their decisions being binding and enforceable. (Model E is a sub-case of Model C.)

Model F: There may be one or more than one level of decision-making above individuals and/or households. Indeed there may be many such levels and these may come and go and their constituent units may frequently change. There is a "rule of law" in the sense that many norms exist which govern peoples' rights and obligations once their interaction begins. There is lacking a continuing organizational apparatus for making decisions or a political apparatus having a specified membership. There exists, instead, the appreciation by participants that they are more closely linked by kinship or territorial proximity to some of their fellows than to others. When in need of collaborators, they call first upon these "neighbors" for help. There may be no normative rule specifying that such requests should be honored. There are, however, strong pressures upon "neighbors" to assist if they are later to mobilize assistance for themselves and there are, once assistance is contemplated, norms governing the establishment and operation of these ad hoc relationships. The ethnographer is likely to report such things as the following: there is no means of making binding decisions or of enforcing decisions that are made; the people are highly individualistic, perhaps irascibly so.

**If central organization of government is that described in Model C or in Model D, specify whether the relation of that central organization to intermediate levels of government or to the smaller units of government most closely resembles one of the models under A, Model B, or Model F. Specify and describe.

Model G: This category is different from F in that (1) there exist routinized and rather frequent occasions on which the body politic or large segments of it assemble and on which a collective focus and perhaps a collective sentiment can emerge. This category also differs from D in that it (2) consists of a direct democracy, not of representatives. It differs from E in that (3) no binding decisions are made and (4) there is no existing practice or apparatus for implementing collective decisions.

The occasions on which the body politic gathers may have a routine locale: a specific time or place for meeting may exist – a plaza where men gather after dinner, a well, a sweathouse. These occasions have aspects of a town meeting: there is a physical assemblage and not merely an informal network of interpersonal obligations. There may be a collective task involved (e.g., cleaning the village, repairing boats) or none at all. Moreover, (5) there is some stable collective organization (e.g., village, clan) within which these occasions occur: They are not ad hoc alliances. Participation in the occasion is in some measure a matter of ascriptive right if not of ascriptive duty. An individual's or a family's membership is not solely contingent on his choosing to participate: he has a right as a member of a larger whole.

VII. CODE: OTHER TOPICS

A. Unlegitimated Conquest States
   0. Conquest state. One society has conquered another, the conquerors settling down among the conquered and gaining most of their livelihood from their subjects. The conquerors obtain tribute and/or services from the subject population and exercise controls necessary to prevent rebellions. The conquerors do not establish institutionalized procedures for obtaining advice and/or consent from the subject population or for limiting the demands they may make on subjects (e.g., legal standards, religious standards, organizations to protect civil rights).
   1. Not a conquest state.

B. Society-Wide organizations sponsored by the polity
   0. Present. These are groups organized on a society-wide basis rather than existing merely in each of several sub-populations. Thus there sometimes are military units (e.g., age-regiments), religious organizations, educational systems, etc. that have a national or other society-wide organization that cuts across the population's division into territorial or kin units. Indicate

what the relevant organizations are and who belongs to them.
1. Absent.

C. Society-Wide organizations independent of the polity
0. Present. The nature of these organizations is identical with those sketched above except: (a) an office in government does not automatically give one a particular office in the independent organization or vice versa and (b) the independent organization has some considerable autonomies, as, for example, in conferring membership, certifying to advanced statuses of training or performance, determining its program, disciplining its members, representing its members to outside groups. Indicate what the relevant organizations are, the evidence for their independence, and who belongs to them.
1. Absent.

D. Economy of the total society
0. Communal. All constituent bodies in the society have by right a claim to a share of the society's total produce. The fulfillment of this claim is provided for in a systematic fashion: A central government regularly (e.g., annually, daily) purchases or otherwise obtains foodstuffs, these to be distributed routinely and by a universalistic criterion to all constituent bodies in the society, these foodstuffs being depended on for sustenance by most or all recipients or all producing units (e.g., individuals, nuclear families) regularly (e.g., annually, daily). Or the government or these units regularly store 25 per cent or more of staple foodstuffs for use by all other constituent bodies in the society, or such units regularly share staple foodstuffs with such constituent bodies. If there is a formal government, it may promote these arrangements by establishing storage facilities, by transporting supplies to needy areas, or by other means.

In a communal economy, these are the normal procedures, not a standby system for possible emergencies.

There is one primitive system that resembles communal practice but is fundamentally different. Ethnographers refer to it as a redistributive system: a governor receives gifts or taxes and is expected generously to give most of what he receives to others. A redistributive system makes distribution depend on the discretion of the governor. It does not provide that each constituent body has "by right a claim to a share of the society's total produce."
1. Not communal. All other arrangements for storage and division of staple foodstuffs.

APPENDIX II

ETHNOGRAPHIC BIBLIOGRAPHY

These notes contain the major references employed for evaluating societies listed in Tables 2 and 4 together with a brief characterization of the polity of each society. Comparable information for societies listed in Table 1 can be found in Swanson, 1968.

Athenians (500 B.C.)
  Becker, Howard
      1950 In Defense of Morgan's "Grecian Gens": Ancient Kinship and Stratification. Southwestern Journal of Anthropology, 6 (Autumn):309-39.
  Finley, Morris I.
      1963 The Ancient Greeks. London: Chatto and Windus.
  Freeman, Kathleen
      1950 Greek City-States. London: Macdonald and Co., Ltd.
  Glotz, Gustav
      1951 The Greek City and Its Institutions. (N. Mallinson, Translator) New York: Alfred A. Knopf.
  Hignett, C.
      1952 A History of the Athenian Constitution to the End of the Fifth Century B.C. Oxford: Clarendon Press.
  Levi, Mario A.
      1965 Political Power in the Ancient World. (Jane Costello, Translator) London: Weidenfeld and Nicolson.

Aztec (Early 15th century)
  Adams, Robert McC.
      1966 The Evolution of Urban Society, Early Mesopotamia and Pre-hispanic Mexico. Chicago: Aldine Publishing Co.
  Katz, Friedrich
      1958 The Evolution of Aztec Society. Past and Present, No. 13 (April):14-25.
  Vaillant, George C.
      1944 Aztecs of Mexico: Origin, Rise and Fall of the Aztec Nation. Garden City: Doubleday, Doran and Co.

Bedouin (Rwala)
  Hitti, Philip K.
      1963 History of the Arabs. London: Macmillan and Co.
  Musil, Alois
      1928 The Manners and Customs of the Rwala Bedouins. New York: American Geographical Society.

Buduma

Bouillié, Robert
    1937 Les Coutumes Familiales au Kanem. Études de Sociologie et d'Ethnologie Juridiques, 24.

Burmese (circa 1800)

Cady, John F.
    1958 A History of Modern Burma. Ithaca: Cornell University Press.

Hall, G. E.
    1956 Burma, London: Hutchinson's University Library.

Harvey, G. E.
    1925 History of Burma from the Earliest Times to 10 March 1824 the Beginning of the English Conquest. London: Longmans, Green and Co.

Cágaba

Park, Willard Z.
    1948 Tribes of the Sierra Nevada de Santa Marta, Colombia. In: Steward, Julian H., ed., Handbook of South American Indians, Vol. 2, pp. 865-86. Washington, D.C.: U.S. Government Printing Office.

Cambodians (18th century)

Coedés, Georges
    1964 Les États Hindouises D'Indochine et D'Indonésie. Paris: E. de Boccard.

Hall, Daniel G.E.
    1964 A History of South-East Asia. London: Macmillan and Co., Ltd.

Heine-Geldern, Robert
    1948 Conceptions of State and Kinship in Southeast Asia. Data Paper No. 18, Southeast Asia Program, Cornell University.

Leclère, Adhémard
    1894 Recherches sur le droit public des Cambodgiens. Paris: Augustin Challamel.

Cashinawa

Metraux, Alfred
    1948 Tribes of the Jurua-Purus Basins. In: Steward, Julian H., ed., Handbook of South American Indians, Vol. 3, pp. 657-86. Washington, D.C.: U.S. Government Printing Office.

Chinese (Ming dynasty)

Reischauer, Edwin O. and John K. Fairbank
    1958 East Asia, The Great Tradition. Boston: Houghton Mifflin Co.

Van der Sprenkel, Otto
    1964 Max Weber on China. History and Theory, 3 (3):348-70.

Van der Sprenkel, Sybil
    1962 Legal Institutions in Manchu China, A Sociological Analysis. London: Athlone Press.

Weber, Max
    1951 The Religion of China, Confucianism and Taoism. (Hans H. Gerth, Translator) Glencoe: Free Press.

Dinka

Lienhardt, Godfrey
    1958 The Western Dinka. In Middleton, John, and David Tait, eds., Tribes Without Rulers: Studies in African Segmentary Systems, pp. 97-135. New York: Humanities Press.
    1961 Divinity and Experience: The Religion of the Dinka. New York: Oxford University Press.

Egyptians (Middle Kingdom)

Gardiner, Alan H.
    1961 Egypt of the Pharaohs, An Introduction. Oxford: Clarendon Press.

Wilson, John A.
    1951 The Burden of Egypt, An Interpretation of Ancient Egyptian Culture. Chicago: University of Chicago Press.

Fulani

Stenning, Derrick J.
    1959 Savannah Nomads, A Study of the Wodaabe Pastoral Fulani of Western Bornu Province, Northern Region, Nigeria. London: Oxford University Press.

Havasupai

Spier, Leslie
    1928 Havasupai Ethnography. Anthropological Papers of The American Museum of Natural History, Vol. 29.

Hebrews (Solomon's Kingdom)

Albright, William F.
    1957 From the Stone Age to Christianity, Monotheism and the Historical Process. Garden City: Doubleday.

Johnson, Aubrey R.
    1955 Sacral Kingship in Ancient Israel. Cardiff: University of Wales Press.

Oesterley, W. O. E., and Theodore H. Robinson
    1932 A History of Israel, Vol. 1. Oxford: Clarendon Press.

Pedersen, Johannes
    1946 Israel, Its Life and Culture, 2 Vols. London: Oxford University Press.

De Vaux, Roland
    1961 Ancient Israel, Its Life and Institutions. (John McHugh, Translator) New York: McGraw-Hill.

Weber, Max
    1952 Ancient Judaism. (Hans H. Gerth and Don Martindale, Translators) Glencoe: Free Press.

Hottentot

Schapera, Isaac
    1930 The Khoisan Peoples of South Africa: Bushmen and Hottentots. London: Routledge and Sons.

Iban
>   Freeman, J.D.
>> 1955 Iban Agriculture, A Report on the Shifting Cultivation of Hill Rice by the Iban of Sarawak. London: Her Majesty's Stationery Office.
>> 1958 The Family System of the Iban of Borneo. Cambridge Papers in Anthropology, No. 1, pp. 15-52.
>> 1960 The Iban of Western Borneo. In: Murdock, George P., ed., Social Structure in Southeast Asia. Viking Fund Publications in Anthropology, No. 29, pp. 65-87.
>   Tar Haar, Barend
>> 1948 Adat Law in Indonesia. (George C.O. Haas and Margaret Hordyk, Translators) New York: Institute of Pacific Relations.

Ifugao
>   Barton, Roy F.
>> 1919 Ifugao Law. University of California Publications in American Archaeology and Ethnology, 15 (1):1-186.
>> 1922 Ifugao Economics. University of California Publications in American Archaeology and Ethnology, 15 (5):385-446.
>> 1946 The Religion of the Ifugaos. Memoirs of the American Anthropological Association, No. 65.
>   Hoebel, E. Adamson
>> 1954 The Law of Primitive Man, A Study in Comparative Legal Dynamics, pp. 101-09. Cambridge: Harvard Press.

Inca (Imperial period)
>   Means, Philip A.
>> 1936 Ancient Civilizations of the Andes. New York: Charles Scribner's Sons.
>   Murra, John V.
>> 1967 On Inca Political Structure. In: Cohen, Ronald and John Middleton, eds., Comparative Political Systems, pp. 339-53. Garden City: Natural History Press.

Iranians (Sassanid period)
>   Christensen, Arthur
>> 1907 L'Empire des Sassanides: Le Peuple, L'État, La Cour. Copenhagen: Bianco Lunos Bogtykkeri.
>> 1936 L'Iran sous les Sassanides. Copenhagen: Levin and Munksgaard.
>   Christensen, Arthur and W. Ensslin
>> 1956 Sassanid Persia. In: The Cambridge Ancient History, Vol. 12, pp. 110-17. Cambridge University Press.
>   Duchesne-Guillemin, Jacques
>> 1962 La Religion de L'Iran Ancien. Paris: Presses Universitaires de France.
>   Huart, Clement
>> 1927 Ancient Persia and Iranian Civilization. (M.R. Dobie, Translator) New York: Alfred A. Knopf.
>   Nyberg, Henrik S.
>> 1938 Die Religionen des alten Iran. Leipzig: J.C. Hinrichs.

Olmstead, Albert T.
>1948 History of the Persian Empire, Achaemenid Period. Chicago, University of Chicago Press.

Rawlinson, George
>1882 The Seventh Great Oriental Monarchy or the Geography, History, and Antiquities of the Sassanian or New Persian Empire, Vol. 2. New York: Dodd, Mead and Co.

Wikander, Stig
>1946 Die Feuerpriester in Klein-asien und Iran. Lund: C. W. K. Gleerup.

Zaehner, Robert C.
>1956 The Teachings of the Magi. London: George Allen and Unwin.
>1961 The Dawn and Twilight of Zoroastrianism. London: Weidenfeld and Nicolson.

Japanese (Tokugawa period)

Bellah, Robert N.
>1957 Tokugawa Religion. Glencoe: The Free Press.

Dore, R. P.
>1965 Education in Tokugawa Japan. London: Routledge and Kegan Paul.

Hall, John W.
>1962 Feudalism in Japan, A Reassessment. Comparative Studies in Society and History, 5, (October):15-51.
>1966 Government and Local Power in Japan: 500 to 1700, A Study Based on Bizen Province. Princeton: Princeton University Press.

Reischauer, Edwin O.
>1956 Japanese Feudalism. In: Coulborn, Rushton, ed., Feudalism in History, pp. 26-48. Princeton: Princeton University Press.

Reischauer, Edwin O. and John K. Fairbank
>1960 East Asia, The Great Tradition. Boston: Houghton Mifflin Co.

Sansom, George B.
>1958 A History of Japan, 2 Vols. Stanford: Stanford University Press.

Javanese (circa 1800 A.D.)

Raffles, Thomas S.
>1965 The History of Java, Vol. 1. London: Oxford University Press (originally published in 1817).

Shrieke, Bertram J.O.
>1955 Indonesian Sociological Studies. Selected Writings of B. Schrieke. The Hague: W. van Hoeve Ltd.

Van Leur, J.C.
>1955 Indonesian Trade and Society, Essays in Asian Social and Economic History. The Hague: W. van Hoeve Ltd.

Wertheim, Willem F.
>1956 Indonesian Society in Transition, A Study of Social Change. The Hague: W. van Hoeve Ltd.

Jukun
  Meek, Charles K.
    1931 A Sudanese Kingdom, An Ethnographical Study of the Jukun-speaking Peoples of Nigeria. London: Kegan Paul, Trench, Trubner, and Co.

Kalmuk
  Aberle, David F.
    1953 The Kinship System of the Kalmuk Mongols. University of New Mexico Publications in Anthropology, No. 8, pp. 1-48.
  Krader, Lawrence
    1963 Social Organization of the Mongol-Turkic Pastoral Nomads. The Hague: Mouton and Co.
  Vladimirtsov, B.
    1948 Le Régime Social des Mongols. (Michel Carsow, Translator) Publications due Musée Guimet, Bibliotheque d'Études, Vol. 52.

Kazak
  Hudson, Alfred E.
    1938 Kazak Social Structure. Yale University Publications in Anthropology, No. 20.
  Krader, Lawrence
    1963 Social Organization of the Mongol-Turkic Pastoral Nomads. The Hague: Mouton and Co.
  Murdock, George P.
    1934 Our Primitive Contemporaries. New York: Macmillan, pp. 135-62.

Koreans (Yi dynasty)
  Osgood, C. B.
    1951 The Koreans and Their Culture. New York: Ronald.
  Reischauer, Edwin O., and John K. Fairbank
    1960 East Asia, The Great Tradition. Boston: Houghton Mifflin Co.

Lapps
  Whitaker, Ian
    1955 Social Relations in a Nomadic Lappish Community. Oslo: Utgitt av Norsk Folkemuseum.

Lugbara
  Middleton, John
    1958 The Political System of the Lugbara of the Nile-Congo Divide. In Middleton, John and David Tait, eds., Tribes without Rulers, Studies in African Segmentary Systems, pp. 203-29. London: Routledge and Kegan Paul.
    1960 Lugbara Religion, Ritual and Authority among an East African People. London: Oxford University Press.
    1965 The Lugbara of Uganda. New York: Holt, Rinehart and Winston.

Marquesans

Linton, Ralph
1939 Marquesan Culture. In: Kardiner, Abram, ed., The Individual and His Society, The Psychodynamics of Primitive Social Organization, pp. 137-96. New York: Columbia University Press.

Maya (Period of Spanish conquest)

Carrasco, Pedro
1967 The Civil Religious Hierarchy in Meso American Communities: Pre-Spanish Background and Colonial Development. In: Cohen, Ronald, and John Middleton, eds., Comparative Political Systems: Studies in the Politics of Pre-Industrial Societies, pp. 397-414. Garden City: Natural History Press.

Chamberlain, Robert S.
1951 The Pre-Conquest Tribute and Service System of the Maya as Preparation for the Spanish Repartimiento-Ecomienda in Yucatan. University of Miami Hispanic-American Studies, No. 10.

Roys, Ralph L.
1943 The Indian Background of Colonial Yucatan. Washington D.C.: Carnegie Institution of Washington.
1957 The Political Geography of the Yucatan Maya. Washington, D.C.: Carnegie Institution of Washington.

Von Hagen, Victor W.
1957 The Ancient Sun Kingdoms of the Americas. Cleveland: The World Publishing Co.

Natchez

Hart, C. W. M.
1943 A Reconsideration of the Natchez Social Structure. American Anthropologist, 45, (July-September):374-86.

MacLeod, William C.
1924 Natchez Political Evolution. American Anthropologist, 26, (April-June): 201-29.

Swanton, John R.
1911 Indian Tribes of the Lower Mississippi Valley and Adjacent Coast of the Gulf of Mexico. Bureau of American Ethnology, Bulletin 43.

Tooker, Elisabeth
1963 Natchez Social Organization: Fact or Anthropological Folklore? Ethnohistory, 10 (Fall):358-72.

Ngoni (Mpezeni)

Barnes, James A.
1954 Politics in a Changing Society, A Political History of the Fort Jameson Ngoni. London: Oxford University Press.

Nicobarese

Man, Edward H.
1888 The Nicobar Islanders. The Journal of the Anthropological Institute of Great Britain and Ireland, 18(4):354-94.

Whitehead, George
    1924 In the Nicobar Islands. London: Seeley, Service and Co. Ltd.

Nuer

Evans-Pritchard, E. E.
    1940 The Nuer. Oxford: Oxford University Press.
    1940 The Nuer of Southern Sudan. In: Fortes, Meyer, and E. E. Evans-Pritchard, eds., African Political Systems. London: Oxford University Press, pp. 272-96.

Nyoro

Richards, Audrey I., ed.
    1960 East African Chiefs, A Study of Political Development in some Uganda and Tanganyika Tribes. London: Faber and Faber Ltd.

Roscoe, John
    1923 The Bakitara or Banyoro. Cambridge: Cambridge University Press.

Pawnee (Skidi)

Dorsey, George A. and James R. Murie
    1940 Notes on Skidi Pawnee Society. Anthropological Series, Field Museum of Natural History, Vol. 27, pp. 65-119.

Hyde, George E.
    1951 Pawnee Indians. Denver: University of Denver Press.

Lounsbury, Floyd G.
    1956 A Semantic Analysis of the Pawnee Kinship Usage. Language, 32 (January-March):157-94.

Murie, James R.
    1914 Pawnee Indian Societies. Anthropological Papers of the American Museum of Natural History, Vol. 11, Part 7, pp. 543-644.

Penobscot

Speck, Frank G.
    1940 Penobscot Man, The Life History of a Forest Tribe in Maine. Philadelphia: University of Pennsylvania Press.

Romans (Principate)

Boak, Arthur E. R., and W. G. Sinnigen
    1965 History of Rome 565 B.C. New York: Macmillan Co.

Carcopino, Jerome
    1940 Daily Life in Ancient Rome, The People and the City at the Height of the Empire. (E.O. Lorimer, Translator) New Haven: Yale University Press.

Rostovtzeff, M.I.
    1926 The Social and Economic History of the Roman Empire. Oxford: The Clarendon Press.

Weber, Max
    1950 The Social Causes of the Decay of Ancient Civilization. (Christian Mackauer, Translator) Journal of General Education, 5 (October):75-88.

APPENDIX II

Sinhalese (Kandyan period)
  Ariyapala, M.B.
    1956 Society in Medieval Ceylon. Colombo: K.V.G. de Silva.
  Codrington, H.W.
    1926 A Short History of Ceylon. London: Macmillan and Co.
  D'Oyly, John
    1929 A Sketch of the Constitution of the Kandyan Kingdom. Colombo: Government Printer, Ceylon.
  Leach, Edmund R.
    1959 Hydraulic Society in Ceylon. Past and Present, No. 15 (April):2-26.
  Murphey, Rhoads
    1957 The Ruin of Ancient Ceylon. Journal of Asian Studies, 16 (February): 181-200.
  Pieris, R.
    1956 Sinhalese Social Organization. Colombo: Ceylon University Press Board.
  Ryan, Bryce
    1953 Caste in Modern Ceylon. New Brunswick: Rutgers University Press.
  Singer, Marshall R.
    1964 The Emerging Elite. A Study of Political Leadership in Ceylon. Cambridge: Massachusetts Institute of Technology Press.

Subanun
  Christie, Emerson B.
    1909 The Subanuns of Sindangan Bay. Bureau of Science Division of Ethnology Publications, Vol. 6, Part 1. Manila.
  Frake, Charles O.
    1960 The Eastern Subanun of Mindanao. In: Murdock, George P., ed., Social Structure in Southeast Asia. Viking Fund Publications in Anthropology, No. 29 pp. 51-64.

Swazi
  Kuper, Hilda
    1947 An African Aristocracy, Rank among the Swazi. London: Oxford University Press.
    1952 The Swazi. London: International African Institute.

Taino
  Loven, Sven
    1935 Origins of the Tainan Culture, West Indies. Goteborg: Elanders Bokfryckeri Akfiebolag.

Tewa (San Ildefonso)
  Dozier, Edward P.
    1954 The Hopi-Tewa of Arizona. University of California Publications in American Archaeology and Ethnology, 44(3):259-376.

    1961 Rio Grande Pueblos. In: Spicer, Edward H., ed., Perspectives in American Indian Culture Change, pp. 94-186. Chicago: University of Chicago Press.

Parsons, Elsie C.
    1927 The Social Organization of the Tewa of New Mexico. Memoirs of the American Anthropological Association, No. 35, pp. 1-309.

Whitman, William
    1947 The Pueblo Indians of San Ildefonso. New York: Columbia University Press.

Thai (18th century)

Thompson, Virginia M.
    1941 Thailand, The New Siam. New York: The Macmillan Co.

Wales, Horace G. Q.
    1934 Ancient Siamese Government and Administration. London: Bernard Quaritch, Ltd.

Tibetans (1900-1950 A.D.)

Bell, Charles
    1924 Tibet, Past, and Present. Oxford: The Clarendon Press.
    1928 The People of Tibet. Oxford: The Clarendon Press.

Cammann, Schuyler
    1951 Trade Through the Himalayas, The Early British Attempts to Open Tibet. Princeton: Princeton University Press.

Carrasco, Pedro
    1959 Land and Polity in Tibet. Seattle: University of Washington Press.

Waddell, L.A.
    1939 The Buddhism of Tibet, or Lamaism. Cambridge: Cambridge University Press.

Tongans

Gifford, Edward W.
    1929 Tongan Society. Honolulu: Bernice P. Bishop Museum.

Trumai

Murphy, Robert F. and Buell Quain
    1955 The Trumai Indians of Central Brazil. Monographs of the American Ethnological Society, 24.

Tuareg

Dueyrier, Henri
    1864 Les Touareg du Nord. Paris: Challemel Ainé.

Nicolaisen, Johannes
    1963 Ecology and Culture of the Pastoral Tuareg with Particular Reference to the Tuareg of Ahaggar and Ayr. Copenhagen: The National Museum.

Tupinamba

Metraux, Alfred
    1948 The Tupinamba. In: Steward, Julian H., ed., Handbook of South American Indians, Vol. 3, pp. 95-133. Washington, D.C.: U.S. Government Printing Office.

Ulawans
Ivens, Walter G.
- 1927 Melanesians of the South-east Solomon Islands. London: Kegan Paul, Trench, Trubner and Co., Ltd.

Vietnamese (18th century)
Burling, Robbins
- 1965 Hill Farms and Padi Fields, Life in Mainland Southeast Asia. Englewood Cliffs: Prentice-Hall, Inc.

Buttinger, Joseph
- 1958 The Smaller Dragon, A Political History of Vietnam. New York: Frederick A. Praeger.

Coedes, Georges
- 1965 The Making of South East Asia. (H.M. Wright, Translator) Berkeley: University of California Press, Part 2, Chapter 1; Part 5, Chapter 5.

Wapishana
Farabee, William C.
- 1918 The Central Arawaks. University of Pennsylvania Anthropological Publications, Vol. 9.

Yaqui (Sonora)
Halden, W. C., et al.
- 1936 Studies of the Yaqui Indians of Sonora Mexico. Texas Technological College Bulletin, 12, No. 1

Spicer, Edward H.
- 1954 A Yaqui Village in Sonora. Memoirs of the American Anthropological Association, No. 77, pp. 1-234.

- 1961 Yaqui. In: Spicer, Edward H., ed., Perspectives in American Indian Culture Change, pp. 7-93. Chicago: University of Chicago Press.

Zulu
Gluckman, Max
- 1940 The Kingdom of the Zulu of South Africa. In: Fortes, Meyer and E. E. Evans-Pritchards, eds., African Political Systems, pp. 25-55. London: Oxford University Press.

Krige, Eileen J.
- 1950 The Social System of the Zulus. Pietermaritzburg: Shuter and Shooter.

ETHNOGRAPHIC SUMMARIES

The purpose of these summaries is to present data essential for arriving at a decision about each society's type of regime (see tables 2 and 4). These are not all of the relevant data, but I offer them as consistent with the whole of the data I have examined and sufficient to permit the classification needed. The data are presented as answers to the following six questions:

1. What is the largest indigenous decision-making unit under which these people live?
2. What significant but smaller indigenous decision-making units are found in this population?
3. Who may legitimately play what role in shaping decisions made by the unit specified under 1 above?
4. Who may legitimately play what role in shaping decisions made by the units specified under 2 above, and, especially, what role if any have such units with respect to decisions of the unit specified under 1?
5. Is the economy communal?
6. Are there other critical observations?

To avoid any lengthy repetition, I sometimes use the words "general administration" to refer to the exercise of all or most of the following powers of government: deciding on war or peace, establishing and operating a system of justice, preserving internal order, deploying armed forces, coordinating important economic operations or supplying facilities for them.

PASTORAL SOCIETIES

Bedouin (Rwala)
1. Tribe
2. Clans
3. a. Tribal chief: No information concerning accession to office. Collects taxes. Adjudicates disputes. Leader in deciding on war or peace with other tribes. Apparently not a figure with any great powers or any control over day-to-day government.
   b. Judges: Hereditary in certain families; are often clan chiefs. May overrule judicial decisions of chiefs. There is a formal system of judicial procedure and arbitration employed by judges.
4. Clan chief: Post is hereditary in a particular family; most capable male member succeeds to the post. Leads in war. Passes sentences in civil and criminal cases. Retains post if capable in war and government.
5. Slaves and camels are held as private property.
6. Polity is very fluid, clans attaching themselves to chiefs or warriors who are successful, deposing or leaving those who are not. Clans unite on an ad hoc basis for action as a tribe. Intra-tribal strife common; clans frequently revenging some harm done to a kinsman. Inter-tribal wars also frequent.

Buduma
1. Informal net of obligations
2. Households
3. Leadership beyond the household developed on an ad hoc basis. To conduct a raid, the people concerned were called together and they elected a chief whose powers extended only to this one activity.
4. No detailed description of household polity given.

5. Property is privately held.

Dinka
1. Subtribes
2. Tribal sections, families
3. a. Master of the fishing spear; chief warrior: These two figures are informally acknowledged as preeminent in the pursuit of their specialties within the subtribe. They are also responsible for forming the age-sets. The two chief figures lead by example and because they are respected. Their influence depends on their personal qualities.
   b. Each adult male resident individually: There are no councils or officials; nor are there any routinized procedures for general administration. Leadership is ad hoc.
4. Government of smaller units repeats that just described.
5. No evidence of a communal economy.

Fulani (Wodaabe)
1. Clan
2. Lineage groups; households
3. Clan head: Inherits position. Primarily a ceremonial leader, but in consultation with lineage chiefs can banish from clan anyone who disobeys the customary law.
4. Lineage chief: (During most of the year, lineages follow separate nomadic courses, coming together for ceremonial purposes once a year in the wet season. That is when the clan chief plays his role. During the major part of the year, lineage groups are the significant unit in Fulani life.) The position of lineage chief is hereditary in house of current holder, providing heir is acceptable to adult males of group. Functions mainly advisory. Acts as spokesman for the group. Supervises marriages within the group. General responsibility for coordination of pastoral activities. Office is for life, but people dissatisfied with leader will select a man they prefer and leave old leader.
5. Not a communal economy.

Hottentot
1. Tribe
2. Clans
3. a. Tribal chief: Position hereditary in the senior clan. Leads in defense and presides over tribal council. Can order that certain grazing lands lie fallow; orders people to perform such public work as building roads; receives fines levied in criminal cases; demands tribute from all game caught on tribal land. Must approve all use of capital punishment.
   b. Tribal council: Meets often. Composed of chiefs of component clans. Discusses important issues and acts as court of law. Deals with questions of war and peace, disputes among clans, civil and criminal adjudication, external relations. The major power of the tribe.
4. a. Clan chief: Hereditary position. Presides over clan council. Represents clan on tribal council.
   b. Clan council: All adult members. Deal with all matters of common interest and act as a court of law.
5. Not a communal economy.

Kalmuk (Baga Dorbed)
1. Äämag
2. Hotans; extended families
3. Informal, transient relations among families who have common membership in the population ranging over a particular grazing area. There is a definite conception of membership: of which families are members and which not. The area belongs to the collectivity of members.
4. a. Hotan: an ad hoc group of families. May include one or a few extended families, but component families may be connected simply by friendship or because some are hired laborers of others. A unit often being recomposed as families break away to establish their own hotan and as others join the original group. No over-arching authority except by agreement among independent families that comprise the group.
   b. Extended families: Apparently decisions are made by agreement among all adult males. Senior male lenient and nurturant, this in an effort to make continued affiliation with family attractive to younger married men. Herds held in common, but any head of a nuclear family can take his share and leave.
5. Not a communal economy.

Kazak
1. Clan
2. Sub-clans, auls
3. Clan members have a customary solidarity in avenging injuries inflicted upon their fellows by outsiders, in owning the land over which members graze their herds, and in uniting for defense. But all these arrangements are customary and informal. There is no formal governmental arrangement.
4. a. Chief of sub-clan: An individual who comes informally to be recognized as an able and powerful person and to whom others turn for protection and for the adjudication of disputes. Authority depends solely on his personal abilities. May be chosen by members of other sub-clans to judge disputes.
   b. Headman of aul: Patriarch of largest and wealthiest family among those that journey together in the summer migrations. Powers are like those of chief of sub-clan. Several auls possessing adjoining winter sites and linked by blood or for mutual protection form a sub-clan.
5. All property and produce privately held.

Lapps
1. sii'da (the winter herding unit)
2. Households
3. a. sii'da leader: The man who comes informally to be acknowledged as the most skillful among the heads of the small group of households deciding for the moment to winter together. Authority depends solely on personal qualities. Decides on the pasturage and care of the herds and on the route followed in migration.
   b. Every head of a component household: All are free to leave at any time and membership of groups is very fluid. Leadership, like membership, is purely ad hoc.
4. Household head: Apparently a married son in whom is vested ownership of herds but who must then provide for his dependent parents and unmarried siblings as well as for his wife and children. Represents family in operations of sii'da.
5. Adherence to concept of private property is rigid.

APPENDIX II

Lugbara
1. Tribe
2. Major, minor, minimal lineage segments: most of them localized
3. Tribe is widest area over which there exists a rule of law. Tribe has no general government, kin segments banding together along lines of traditional affinity to form ad hoc units for particular enterprises.
4. Minimal lineage head: Attains post through seniority. Head of several dispersed but neighboring homesteads in which lineage members reside. Controls group's livestock. Decides on hostilities or peace with other groups. Minimal lineage also holds land and daughters in common.
5. Private property held by minimal lineage.

Ngoni (Mpezeni)
1. Paramount chieftaincy
2. Regions; residential segments
3. Paramount chief: Inherits his office. Appoints regional governors and the leaders of the age-regiments. All cattle and captives belong to him. Directs the regiments, each of these consisting of young men from each major residential segment in the country. Paramount and all lesser lords have power over the affairs of their people only if those affairs are referred to them for action by the lord's lieutenants. Any dispute might eventually be referred to the Paramount.
4. a. Regional governor: Appointed by the Paramount. Had privilege of keeping his own captives.
   b. Lords of residential segments of various sizes, some very large: Leading man whose protection and government was sought by others. Segments constantly building up and dissolving. Have their own militia. Control cattle in their districts. Lords of larger segments can shift people from one inferior segment to another.

   Strength of a segment dependent upon its internal cohesion and its relative fighting power. Competition among segments' lords and constant rise of new segments prevents their combining successfully to challenge the Paramount's central power. Lord of a segment responsible politically to the Paramount for the actions of his segment.
   c. Village headman: Controlled local cattle. Village was herding unit.
5. Not a communal economy.

Nuer
1. Tribal sections
2. Villages
3. a. All members of the maximal lineage: Have preeminence but no special privileges or powers.
   b. Each adult male resident individually: There are no councils or officials, nor are there any routinized procedures for general administration. All leadership is ad hoc.
4. Village government repeats that just described.
5. All property is privately held.

Nyoro
1. Kingdom
2. Districts, sub-districts

3. a. King: Inherited position. Had absolute powers. Appointed chiefs of districts and sub-districts; had to provide ceremonial validation for restricted authority traditionally vested in heads of extended groups of agnates; heirs to considerable properties lacked final legitimation of their inheritance until "introduced" to king. Could appoint to any office whom he chose without restriction and could remove appointees at any time. Was highest court of appeal, and the lowliest peasant had the right to appeal a case to the king for his decision. Absolute power of life and death over his subjects.
   b. Royal family: Specified members of the family inherited ritual offices and offices in the operation of the royal household. Thus the king's oldest brother was head of the royal Bito clan, ruling the princes. His official sister ruled the princesses.
   c. Privileged clans: The people were organized into 150 noncorporate and nonlocalized clans, and some of these had traditional rights to supply officials and advisors in the king's household. (These should not be confused with the advisors chosen by the king to operate the national polity. Some such persons might, of course, wield political influence if the king valued their advice or felt it politic to do so.)
4. Apart from the king's own powers, there was no significant political authority below the national level.
5. Not a communal economy.

Swazi

1. Kingdom
2. Principalities, villages
3. a. King: Position hereditary in the royal clan, particular candidate chosen by the Inner Council. Operates general administration except as noted below. Controls the army, acts as supreme judge, disburses wealth to his people, appoints all officers of the central state, and can remove any of them; allots land.
   b. Queen Mother: Chosen from a clan other than that of the king's father. Has many independent powers that complement or in some respect circumscribe those of the king: he presides over the highest court and can pronounce death sentences, she is in charge of the second highest court and her councillors may take part in discussions at the king's court; her hut is a sanctuary for any man; the king and queen mother have their own regiments at their personal palaces; he distributes land but she must collaborate to bring sufficient rain; he may take cattle from the royal herds and she may rebuke him for wasting the national wealth; she has custody of the sacred objects of the nation, he has special ritual powers; and so on and on.
   c. Inner Council: Consists of the royal family and those senior princes of the king's lineage as chosen by the king-in-council. Usually includes a few chiefs chosen from nonroyal clans and some influential attendants of the king and queen mother. An informal body, some or all of its members being consulted as the king desires. In practice, however, this is a powerful group. The king relies heavily on the support of his lineage. The senior princes serve as his advisers, teachers, and most fearless critics. The Inner Council may advise, make decisions, and may see that decisions are implemented. May fine the king or queen mother if they violate a law.
   d. General Council: A more formal body. Consists of all chiefs and their leading councillors, prominent headmen, and any adult male who wishes to attend. Anyone may speak. Summoned by the king. Procedure is defined by precedent. Meets at least once or twice a year. Approval of General Council required on any important matter and its decision may not be overridden by the Inner Council. Strong pressures to reach unanimity in decisions.

4. a. Governor of a principality: May or may not be a prince. Appointed by the king or, in the case of formerly independent and hereditary chiefdoms, incumbents inherit their positions if they agree to be loyal to the king and he ratifies their accession. May be dismissed by the king for gross misbehavior. May accept or reject or evict subjects; grant land; operate general administration of district; provide ritual leadership; refer unsettled disputes to the king's courts. Governor's mother and kinsmen form a body analogous to the king's Inner Council; headmen of villages a body analogous to the king's General Council. Councillors rebuke or fine the chief if he infringes his subjects' rights; must approve new regulations; regulate the operation of the local courts.
   b. Village headman: Inherits position. Operates general administration of village. Represents the village in external affairs. In all matters outside his own homestead, must consult two local councils analogous to those of the king and governor.
5. Not a communal economy.

Tuareg

1. Principality
2. Noble tribe and vassal tribes; tribal sections
3. Prince: Head of a noble tribe having vassal tribes. Elected by vassal tribes and may be dismissed by them. Preferred choice of prince being the predecessor's son or sister's son. Prince alone has judicial powers over the vassal tribes. Is supreme judge and supreme political authority. Summons nobles and vassals to fight; collects tribute from vassals; installs chiefs of vassal tribes; has the right to half of all booty; selects his own deputies.
4. a. Chiefs of tribal sections: Elected by fellows to operate general administration of section and represent the section to the tribal chief.
   b. Chiefs of vassal tribes: Installed by prince.
   c. All nobles: Possess public rights and participate in the polity of the noble tribe, that being a direct democracy of all adult males. Serve as police and guardians of principality.
   d. Marabout tribes: Nobles who have abdicated all political roles in favor of great religious authority. Only power is persuasion and respect. Are informal ministers of religion, justice, and public instruction; mediate between individuals, tribes, and confederations.
5. Not a communal economy.

Zulu

1. Kingdom
2. Tribes, wards, homesteads
3. a. King: Inherited position. Operated general administration. Only source of national law but new laws were legitimate only if approved by his council. Powers extended to all free men. Appointed major administrative officials of the central government including a head of the army and a "prime minister."
   b. Council: Composed of princes of royal lineage and of important chiefs, all selected by the king. But the king was supposed to listen to his council's advice and to consult it in all important matters. The record indicates that this was generally done.
4. a. Tribal chiefs: Appointed by the king to have responsibility for the general administration of their districts. Authority only that delegated by king. Each had a council analogous to the king's.

b. Ward Leader: Appointed by tribal chief, usually from among his relatives.
   c. Head of Homestead: Post inherited by oldest competent male adult. Represents homestead to higher authorities. Responsible to them for its good order and for conformity to higher policies.
5. Not a communal economy.

HORTICULTURAL SOCIETIES

Cagaba
1. Village
2. Nuclear families
3. Council of village elders: Adult males meet in the village temple to make decisions. There is a headman and a priest, but neither of these seems to have powers beyond those of the council itself. The council's decisions are binding in at least some cases: offenders (thieves, for example) are publicly punished (e.g., imprisoned, made to do penance).
4. During much of the year, nuclear families are separated from one another, each following a seasonal cycle of migration from one dwelling to another, joining other families for periodic religious ceremonies.
5. Each family works as a unit to cultivate tracts of land it owns.

Cashinawa
1. Localized extended family
2. None
3. Council of all adult males makes the important decisions. There is a headman who holds office for life, but seems to have no powers independent of those of the council. How the headman attains office is not indicated.
4. None
5. The extended family corporately owns the land its members jointly cultivate.

Havasupai
1. Village
2. Extended families
3. Informal, ad hoc meetings of adult males: The men of the village talk over public affairs while lying about in the sweat lodge. Occasionally more formal meetings are called by the chiefs. Chiefs are simply outstanding persons or, in a few cases, persons who inherit their position. They in no case have powers beyond those due to personal ability. There is no case in which a chief can do more, as chief, than try to admonish or persuade. There is no evidence that decisions by chiefs or by the informal council can bind anyone to do anything.
4. Extended families are equalitarian groups, their members jointly owning land and jointly cultivating it.
5. Property is privately owned by those who cultivate it and the cultivators own the produce from their labor.

Iban
1. Longhouse community
2. Extended families
3. a. Headman: An office hereditary in the headman's family. Upholds and administers the customary adat law, but lacks power to enforce it upon parties who resist his decisions. Presides at meetings of adult males.
   b. Council: All adult males meeting on an ad hoc basis to discuss some common problem such as a decision to move to another area or to raid a neighboring community. Meeting seems to have no formal means to make or enforce binding decisions. People described as very individualistic, aggressive, and truculent.
4. Extended families are in many respects autonomous. Each is a corporate group owning its own apartment in the longhouse and owning and cultivating its own land. Economic transactions between families are mostly on a cash-payment basis; there is little informal communal assistance. Families may leave the longhouse at any time and, because each has kin in other communities, such movement is fairly common. While in a given longhouse community, a family's members are under the jurisdiction of the local headman. Perhaps the most important feature of that jurisdiction concerns the ritual status of each family. Although each has its own rites, the ritual status of the whole community is endangered if any family violates the Ibanese customs. The headman is responsible for calling the attention of all to whatever custom requires.
5. As indicated above, land is privately owned by extended families.

Ifugao
1. Hamlet
2. Nuclear families
3. a. Kindred: Houses are usually scattered up and down the valleys forming a dispersed rural hamlet, this inhabited by members of a kindred. The kindred collectively owns the land; it cannot be sold except with the full approval of all members. Members of kindred meet for ritual occasions and, as required, to make decisions about subjects of common concern.
   b. Kindred Head: More a center of the family than a headman. Has no important sanctions at his disposal. In the case of the most serious crimes, however, kindred under leadership of head will punish members of the group.
4. All adults.
5. Economically important property owned corporately by the kindred. There is a great deal of communal labor, especially in the construction and maintenance of the large irrigation and terrace systems upon which the economy depends.

Jukun
1. Kingdom
2. Chiefdoms, extended families
3. a. King: Selected by senior officials. Could legitimately be killed if affairs went badly for a period of seven years. Had formal authority over all free men: There was no appeal from his decisions; held power of life and death over all men; could command the people to work on his fields and repair his palace; could appropriate the major share of all fines levied; could appropriate any property for his own use; exacted tribute from harvests, hunts, and on the occasion of religious celebrations.
   b. Abo: This official was head of the king's councillors. No information on how he

obtained office, but, once in office, he served as the permanent "prime minister." Because the king was regarded as a highly sacred figure, he was surrounded by taboos that prevented his being approached except through the Abo and other councillors, the latter forming a patrician caste. The king was informed only on matters the Abo and councillors wanted him to hear. The Abo transmitted all orders from the king to the people, had the principal voice in the selection of a new king, had at least to consent to the execution of a reigning monarch, disposed of all judicial cases not requiring the king's personal investigation, and might act as the leader in war. He was barred from becoming king.

4. a. Chiefs: Chosen by the districts in which they administered. Had to be formally confirmed by the king. Could be deposed by the king, or with the king's approval, by the people of their district. Conducted the general administration of their districts within the limits set by the king's orders, those limits allowing a wide discretion in many matters.
   b. Executive head of kindred and local priest: Executive heads apparently obtained their titles from the district chief. Subordinate to local priest in religious matters.
5. Not a communal economy.

Marquesans

1. Tribe
2. Households
3. a. Chief: How office obtained is uncertain. Apparently hereditary, but people will shift their allegiance to another man if a chief is too unpopular. Chief presides at all great ceremonies but has no priestly duties. Never goes to war. Imposes taboos in preparation for ceremonial feasts; announces communal activities; sets time for fishing parties and harvesting; cannot intervene to administer justice but tells parties to a dispute on whose side he and his relatives will intervene if the dispute is not settled. Presides over council.
   b. Council: Consists of all warriors, craftsmen, and heads of household. A man becomes a warrior by taking a head. Meetings frequent but informal. Chief is merely a spokesman or summarizer of council's discussions. Council can make binding decisions on matters of common concern.
4. Head: Headship of polyandrous household inherited through primogeniture. Head organizes economic activities; divides crops gathered by family.
5. Main foods are breadfruit and fish. All breadfruit trees and all gardens are owned by individuals and are transmitted through inheritance. The first of the four annual crops taken from the breadfruit trees, however, is harvested communally and stored for possible use in famine in great communal pits. Similarly, canoes are individually owned, but the catch from fishing is divided on a communal basis and the fishing itself is organized as a communal activity.

Natchez

1. Kingdom
2. Villages
3. a. King: Inherits position by primogeniture. Has absolute power in internal affairs. Operates general administration. Appoints war chiefs and the chiefs of villages, the lesser officials of government. Has arbitrary powers of life and death; may at will deprive anyone of his property or requisition his labor. Commands all chiefs of villages. Abjectly venerated by commoners.

b. Council: Replaces king as first authority in time of war and in dealings with other societies. Has no power in internal affairs. Composed of the oldest and most capable warriors. King merely sits in their meetings as a witness to the proceedings.
4. Chiefs: Headships of villages thought to be hereditary. Occupied by members of the royal family. Nine to twelve villages.
5. Planting and harvesting are communal activities by all members of a village. Land apparently held by individuals or households.
6. Royal family matrilineal.

Nicobarese
1. Village
2. Households
3. a. Headman: Has little power. Must carry elders with him to take an action.
   b. Council: Consists of village elders. Can decree that a man be killed or punished and has the power to implement such orders.
4. No data
5. Planting is a communal activity, but land is apparently owned or controlled by single individuals. The latter is not clearly described. Villagers live much of the year in hamlets near their fields. In each hamlet all houses "belong" to one man (whether as an individual owner or as the representative of a larger kin group is unclear). Several families live in each house and the leading man feeds all their members.

Pawnee (Skidi)
1. Tribe
2. Villages
3. a. Four priests of tribe's sacred bundles: Hereditary post. Each of the four in rotation is in charge of the people's welfare for one year. While in charge is final source of appeal in disputes. All acts of the council of chiefs must be referred to him. Organizes the buffalo hunt. Chooses war leader.
   b. Chiefs: Hereditary heads of villages. Together constitute a tribal council. Elect additional participants in the council. With agreement of current chief priest can take binding actions.
4. Village chiefs: Inherit position through primogeniture. Sit on tribal council. Appoint assistants with whose help village is administered: order preserved, laws executed, ceremonies prepared, fields allotted to families, disputes resolved.
5. Each village owns the fields its members cultivate.

Penobscot
1. Chiefdom
2. Households
3. a. Chief: Evidence conflicting on procedure by which office was attained, election by the people and inheritance both mentioned. Had little authority. Private justice only means known, but chief's approval necessary for it to be legitimate.
   b. Council: All inhabitants might attend and participate.
4. Households: Families inherit hunting territories and fishing territories inalienable. During most of the year families are separated, gathering food from their own lands. Spend midwinter together at the tribal rendezvous at Oldtown, Maine. At rendezvous, practice

of sharing food between families is the standard: practically all game brought into the village given away to others.
5. See 4 above.

Taino
1. Village
2. Households
3. a. Chief (cacique): Post inherited through primogeniture. Exclusive control in judicial matters. Represented people in external relations. Owned powerful idols. Presided over council of warriors.
   b. Council of warriors: Warriors were an endogamous class standing below the caciques but above the commoners. Assembled under the cacique to decide on important questions such as war and peace. Under cacique's leadership directed agricultural work by commoners.
4. Structure not reported.
5. Data on economy inadequate but appears to involve a collectivized agriculture.

Tewa (San Ildefonso)
1. Village
2. Ceremonial societies
3. a. Summer chief: Elected by the summer moiety for a life term. Cannot deal with temporal affairs. Nominates a governor each year to carry on extra-religious affairs.
   b. Governor: Nominated by summer chief but must be confirmed by the vote of the Principales (all former governors) and the Council (all adult males). Serves for one or a few years. Must be reelected annually. His orders on communal cooperation have to be obeyed. Settles disputes between individuals, responsible for keeping order, sits with other senior pueblo officials (the Principales?) to try cases of misdemeanor, crime, witchcraft. Oversees digging of irrigation ditches and cleaning of pueblo before ceremonies. Controls community funds. Directs policy in external relations. Chairs the council of Principales and senior officers who sit as an executive committee and as a court to settle temporal questions.
   c. Council of Principales and senior officers: Apart from the Principales, senior officers apparently include the governor's assistants: a right-hand man, a left-hand man, a war captain, perhaps others. War captain is elected annually by all adult males. May be reelected repeatedly. Heads police activities.
   d. Council of all adult males: Elects most pueblo officials. Debates matters of importance.
4. No description given of household polity.
5. Agricultural land, cattle, horses, and houses held by individuals as private property. Male and female children inherit equally from their parents.

Tongans (late 19th century)
1. Kingdom
2. Chiefdoms
3. King: Chosen by chiefs. Owns all land and produce. Has certain powers over all men. Head of army and navy. Receives a portion of all produce, all pigs above a certain size, all great fish. Supervises the chiefs. Supervises agriculture and fishing.
4. Chiefs: Inherit position and lands through primogeniture. Appoint their own assistants.

Commoners cannot leave the land of their chief. Chiefs have right to a portion of first fruits; exercise high and low justice; can take from their tenants any property they desire; can arbitrarily order that a tenant be killed.
5. Land and produce "owned" by king and chiefs.

Trumai
1. Village
2. Nuclear families
3. a. Chief and two sub-chiefs: Posts filled through patrilineal inheritance. But officials have no powers except persuasion.
   b. All adult males sit together every evening; decide on cooperative work. Officials coordinate efforts thus determined.
4. No detailed description of family polity.
5. Individuals own garden plots and the produce therefrom. They clear their own land. There is, however, a routine practice of sharing with unrelated families all cooked food, fish, game, and fruit.

Tupinamba
1. Village
2. Extended family
3. a. Chief: Inherits position patrilineally. Authority undisputed in time of war.
   b. Council: Consists of all older men and all warriors. In times of peace must concur in chief's proposals. Has a definite procedure for conducting meetings and making decisions. Decides concerning agricultural practices, punishment of crimes, war and peace, scheduling of ceremonies.
4. Family headman: Directs daily life of communal house consisting of several related nuclear families. Food and tools shared in house. Head of household implements orders of chief and/or council.
5. Food and tools shared by members of communal house. Sharing by neighbors a strong norm. Persons refusing to share would have their houses burned and would be ostracized.

Ulawans
1. Village
2. Hamlets
3. a. Hamlet chiefs: The villages of Ulawa consist of a number of hamlets, each with a chief of sorts. Other inhabitants of hamlet are junior male members of chief's kindred and commoners who had attached themselves to the chief or married into his family. Chiefs are essentially equal in rank. Serve both as priests and leaders in war. No sharp distinction between chiefs and commoners. Chiefs do not govern village. Government described as conducted by the following of customary behavior or through action of the community as a whole without reference to the chiefs.
   b. Whole community.
4. No detailed description of hamlet polity, but apparently a commensal system.
5. Hamlets have a communal economy. Chief's house and canoe house public facilities in which all men may lounge or sleep.

Wapishana
1. Village
2. Households
3. a. Headman: No information on how position attained. Leads collective expeditions to fish. Welcomes visitors. Takes charge of village dances and hunting parties. Advice sought in all important undertakings.
   b. Whole community: Headman has no powers to implement decisions, but people are described as imbued with a desire to cooperate and avoid competition. No game is played that might put someone at a disadvantage. Community opinion is articulated by the headman and that opinion is the great force controlling individual behavior and community policy.
4. Each of several communal houses contains from one to four related families. Building has a common working place, a common storage space. All men eat in common at one end of the house, the women at the other. In hunting, men must go in groups: no man may carry his own game back to the village.
5. Many communal practices (see above) but no clear evidence of communal economy as defined in code.

Yaqui (Sonora)
1. Village
2. Households
3. a. Governors: Five men. Usually serve once in a one-year term of office. Nominated by the officials of the church. Must be confirmed by a unanimous vote of all adults. Meet at least once a week. Chair meetings of elders and administer decisions made at those meetings.
   b. Mayor: Nominated by officials of church. Must be confirmed by unanimous vote of all adults. Holds post for life (or acceptable behavior). Heads elders. Speaks first on any issue. Must countersign all official letters sent by pueblo.
   c. Elders: Speak as advisors to governors and as spokesmen for the villagers.
   d. Church officials: Men and women become apprentice officials by taking a vow to serve or simply by asking to become apprentices. Church head is the maestro. He and three other maestros lead the prayers, chants, and songs. They hold office for life. The head maestro is selected by his predecessor and confirmed by a vote of all adults in the village. The other maestros gain office through ceremonial confirmation by their predecessors. There are also 12 sacristans, these caring for the church property.
   e. Military officers: Leaders of the military society. Men become members of this society by taking a vow to serve the Virgin of Guadalupe as a soldier or by virtue of their parents' vow made when the men were children and taken by their parents to cure them of a childhood disease. The officers make the society's decisions. They guard the civil authorities, announce village meetings, perform rituals, carry out punishments decreed by the civil authorities, serve as an organized core around which the people rally in time of war.
4. No detailed description presented.
5. Land and herds are owned by individual families. Food is often scarce. There is an elaborately developed system of sharing food with relatives, compadres, and godparents, and through ceremonial feasts, with all members of the village. Persons who take food at fiestas are expected to repay it with twelve times the amount received, this being made possible with the help of kinsmen and ritual kinsmen.

LITERATURE CITED

Aberle, David F.
    1962 Matrilineal Descent in Cross-Cultural Perspective. In: Schneider, David M. and Kathleen Gough, eds., Matrilineal Kinship, pp. 655-727. Berkeley: University of California Press.

Adams, Richard N.
    1960 An Inquiry into the Nature of the Family. In: Dole, Gertrude E., and Robert L. Carneiro, eds., Essays in the Science of Culture in Honor of Leslie A. White, pp. 30-49. New York: Thomas Y. Crowell and Co.

Apter, David E.
    1955 The Gold Coast in Transition. Princeton: Princeton University Press.
    1963 System Process and the Politics of Economic Development. In: Hoselitz, Bert F., and Wilbert E. Moore, eds., Industrialization and Society, pp. 135-58. New York: Unesco-Mouton.

Arkell, A.J.
    1951a The History of Darfur 1200-1700 A.D. (I). Sudan Notes and Records, 32, Part I (June): 37-70.
    1951b The History of Darfur 1200-1700 A.D. (I). Sudan Notes and Records, 32, Part II (December): 207-38.

Axelrod, Morris
    1956 Urban Structure and Social Participation. American Sociological Review 21 (Feb.):13-18.

Beaton, A.C.
    1948 The Fur. Sudan Notes and Records, 29, Part I: 1-39.

Befu, Harumi
    1963 Patrilineal Descent and Personal Kindred in Japan. American Anthropologist, 65 (December):1328-41.

Befu, Harumi and Leonard Plotnicov
    1962 Types of Corporate Unilineal Descent Groups. American Anthropologist, 64 (April):313-27.

Bellah, Robert N.
    1964 Religious Evolution. American Sociological Review, 29 (June):358-74.

Brown, James S.
    1952 The Conjugal Family and the Extended Family Group. American Sociological Review, 17 (June):297-306.

Burgess, Ernest W. and Harvey J. Locke
    1950 The Family: From Institution to Companionship. New York: American Book Company.

Coulborn, Rushton
    1958 The State and Religion: Iran, India, and China. Comparative Studies in Society and History, 1 (October):44-57.

Coulborn, Rushton, et al.
    1959 Debate: The State and Religion. Comparative Studies in Society and History, 1 (June):383-93.

Cumming, Elaine and David M. Schneider
    1961 Sibling Solidarity: A Property of American Kinship. American Anthropologist, 63 (June):498-507.

D'Andrade, Roy G.
    1966 Sex Differences and Cultural Institutions. In: Maccoby, Eleanor, ed., The Development of Sex Differences, pp. 174-204. Stanford: Stanford University Press.

Davenport, William
    1959 Nonunilinear Descent and Descent Groups. American Anthropologist, 61 (August):557-72.

Dole, Gertrude E.
    1960 The Classification of Yankee Nomenclature in the Light of Evolution in Kinship. In: Dole, Gertrude E., and Robert L. Carneiro, eds., Essays in the Science of Culture in Honor of Leslie A. White, pp. 162-78. New York: Thomas Y. Crowell and Co.

Eisenstadt, S. N.
    1955 From Generation to Generation. Glencoe: The Free Press.
    1959 Primitive Political Systems: A Preliminary Comparative Analysis. American Anthropologist, 61 (April):200-20.
    1962 Religious Organizations and Political Process in Centralized Empires. The Journal of Asian Studies, 21 (May):271-94.

Ember, Melvin and Carol R. Baldwin
    n.d. The Conditions that Favor Matrilocal and Patrilocal Residence. Unpublished paper, 1965. Department of Anthropology, Antioch College.

Farber, Bernard
    1964 Family: Organization and Interaction. San Francisco: Chandler Publishing Co.
    1966 Kinship Laterality and the Emotionally Disturbed Child. In: Farber, Bernard, ed., Kinship and Family Organization, pp. 69-78. New York: John Wiley and Sons, Inc.

Felkin, Robert W.
    1885 Notes on the Fur (sic!) Tribe of Central Africa. Proceedings of the Royal Society of Edinburgh, 13 (July):205-65.

Firth, Raymond
    1961 Family and Kin Ties in Britain and their Social Implications. British Journal of Sociology, 12 (December):305-09.

Fortes, Meyer
    1953 The Structure of Unilineal Descent Groups. American Anthropologist, 55 (January-March):17-41.

Fortes, Meyer and E. E. Evans-Pritchard, eds.
    1940 African Political Systems. London: Oxford University Press.

LITERATURE CITED

Freeman, J.D.
    1961 On the Concept of the Kindred. The Journal of the Royal Anthropological Institute, 91 (July-December):192-220.

Fried, Morton H.
    1957 The Classification of Corporate Unilineal Descent Groups. The Journal of the Royal Anthropological Institute, 87 (January-June):1-29.

Friedrich, Paul
    1966 Proto-Indo-European Kinship. Ethnology, 5 (January):1-36.

Gamble, David P.
    1957 The Wolof of Senegambia. London: International African Institute.

Garigue, Philip
    1956 French Canadian Kinship and Urban Life. American Anthropologist, 58 (December):1090-1101.

Goody, Jack
    1959 Indo-European Society. Past and Present, 16 (November):88-92.

Gough, Kathleen
    1962a Nayar: Central Kerala. In: Schneider, David M. and Kathleen Gough, eds., Matrilineal Kinship, pp. 298-384. Berkeley: University of California Press.
    1962b Nayar: North Kerala. In: Schneider, David M. and Kathleen Gough, eds., Matrilineal Kinship, pp. 385-404. Berkeley: University of California Press.

Hagstrom, Warren O. and Jeffrey K. Hadden
    1965 Sentiment and Kinship Terminology in American Society. Journal of Marriage and the Family, 27 (August):324-32.

Hinsley, F.H.
    1966 Sovereignty. London: C.A. Watts and Co.

Hobhouse, Leonard T., G.C. Wheeler, and Morris Ginsberg
    1915 The Material Culture and Social Institutions of the Simpler Peoples. London: Chapman and Hall.

Ikawa, Fumiko
    1964 Comments on Befu's 'Patrilineal Descent and Personal Kindred in Japan.' American Anthropologist, 66 (October):1159-62.

Lampen, G.D.
    1950 History of Darfur. Sudan Notes and Records, 31, Part II (December): 177-209.

Lancaster, Lorraine
    1961 Some Conceptual Problems in the Study of Family and Kin Ties in the British Isles. British Journal of Sociology, 12 (December):317-33.

Leach, Edmund
    1962 A Note on the Mangaian Kopu with Special Reference to the Concept of Nonunilineal Descent. American Anthropologist, 64 (June):601-04.

Lewis, Lionel S.
    1963 Kinship Terminology for the American Parent. American Anthropologist, 65 (June):649-52.

Litwak, Eugene
- 1960a Geographic Mobility and Family Cohesion. American Sociological Review, 25 (June):385-94.
- 1960b Occupational Mobility and Family Cohesion. American Sociological Review, 25 (February):9-21.

Mitchell, J.C.
- 1961 Social Change and the Stability of African Marriage in Northern Rhodesia. In: Southall, Aidan, ed., Social Change in Modern Africa, pp. 316-29. London: Oxford University Press.

Mitchell, William E.
- 1965 The Kindred and Baby Bathing in Academe. American Anthropologist, 67 (August):977-85.

Murdock, George P.
- 1937 Correlations of Matrilineal and Patrilineal Institutions. In: Murdock, George P., ed., Studies in the Science of Society, 445-70. New Haven: Yale University Press.
- 1949 Social Structure. New York: The Macmillan Co.
- 1957 World Ethnographic Sample. American Anthropologist, 59 (August): 664-87.
- 1960 Cognatic Forms of Social Organization. Viking Fund Publications in Anthropology, 29:1-14.
- 1964 The Kindred. American Anthropologist, 66 (February):129-32.

Ogburn, William F.
- 1929 The Changing Family. Publications of the American Sociological Society, Vol. 23:124-33.

Parsons, Talcott
- 1943 The Kinship System of the Contemporary United States. American Anthropologist, 45 (January-March):22-38.
- 1951 The Social System. Glencoe: The Free Press.
- 1955a The American Family: Its Relation to Personality and to the Social Structure. In: Parsons, Talcott and Robert F. Bales, eds., Family, Socialization and Interaction Process, pp. 3-33. Glencoe: The Free Press.
- 1955b Family Structure and the Socialization of the Child. In: Parsons, Talcott and Robert F. Bales, eds., Family, Socialization, and Interaction Process, pp. 35-131. Glencoe: The Free Press.
- 1960 Some Ingredients of a General Theory of Formal Organization. In: Parsons, Talcott, Structure and Process in Modern Societies, pp. 59-96. Glencoe: the Free Press.
- 1964 Evolutionary Universals in Society. American Sociological Review, 29 (June):339-57.
- 1966 Societies: Evolutionary and Comparative Perspectives. Englewood Cliffs: Prentice Hall, Inc.

Parsons, Talcott, Robert F. Bales, and Edward Shils
- 1953 Working Papers in the Theory of Action. Glencoe: The Free Press.

Parsons, Talcott and Neil Smelser
    1956 Economy and Society. Glencoe: The Free Press.

Radcliffe-Brown, A. R.
    1935 Patrilineal and Matrilineal Succession. Iowa Law Review, 20:286-303.

Reischauer, Edwin O. and John K. Fairbank
    1958 East Asia, The Great Tradition. Boston: Houghton Mifflin Co.

Richards, Audrey I.
    1940 The Political System of the Bemba Tribe – North Rhodesia. In: Fortes, Meyer, and E. E. Evans-Pritchard, eds., African Political Systems, pp. 83-120. London: Oxford University Press.

Rivers, William H. R.
    1924 Social Organization. New York: A. A. Knopf.

Robbins, Lee N. and Miroda Tomanec
    1962 Closeness to Blood Relatives Outside the Immediate Family. Marriage and Family Living, 24 (November):340-46.

Romney, A. Kimball and Roy G. D'Andrade
    1964 Cognitive Aspects of English Kin Terms. American Anthropologist, 66, Part 2 (June):146-70.

Rossi, Alice S.
    1965 Naming Children in Middle Class Families. American Sociological Review, 30 (August):499-513.

Sabine, George H.
    1950 A History of Political Theory. New York: Henry Holt and Co.

Sahlins, Marshall D.
    1961 The Segmentary Lineage: An Organization of Predatory Expansion. American Anthropologist, 63 (April): 322-45.
    1963 Poor Man, Rich Man, Big-Man, Chief: Political Types in Melanesia and Polynesia. Comparative Studies in Society and History, 5 (April): 285-303.
    1965 On the Ideology and Composition of Descent Groups. Man, No. 95 (July-August):104-07.

Sahlins, Marshall D. and Elman R. Service, eds.
    1960 Evolution and Culture. Ann Arbor: University of Michigan Press.

Schneider, David M. and George C. Homans
    1955 Kinship Terminology and the American Kinship System. American Anthropologist, 57 (December):1194-1208.

Sheffler, H.W.
    1963 A Further Note on the Mangaian Kopu. American Anthropologist, 65: 903-08.

Southall, Aidan W.
    1953 Alur Society: A Study in Processes and Types of Domination. Cambridge: W. Heffer and Sons.

Strayer, Joseph R.
    1958 The State and Religion: An Exploratory Comparison in Different

Cultures: Greece and Rome, The West, Islam. Comparative Studies in Society and History, 1 (October):38-43.

Swanson, Guy E.
- 1960 The Birth of the Gods, The Origin of Primitive Beliefs. Ann Arbor: University of Michigan Press.
- 1967 Religion and Regime, A Sociological Account of the Reformation. Ann Arbor: University of Michigan Press.
- 1968a To Live in Concord with a Society, Two Empirical Studies of Primary Relations. In: Reiss, Albert J., ed., Cooley and Sociological Analysis. Ann Arbor: University of Michigan Press.
- 1968b On Sharing Social Psychology, A Problem in Graduate Education. In: S. Lundstedt, ed., Higher Education in Social Psychology. Cleveland: Case Western Reserve University Press, 1968.

Sweetser, Dorrian A.
- 1963 Asymmetry in Intergenerational Family Relationships. Social Forces, 41 (May):346-52.

Titiev, Mischa
- 1956 The Importance of Space in Primitive Kinship. American Anthropologist, 58 (October):854-65.
- 1957 Addendum to 'Space and Kinship.' American Anthropologist, 59 (August):716.

Wolin, Sheldon S.
- 1960 Politics and Vision: Continuity and Innovation in Western Political Thought. Boston: Little Brown and Co.